How to Escape a Bad Marriage-

A Self Help Divorce Book for Women

Diane Tegarden

FireWalker Publications, Inc.
Pasadena, California

Library of Congress Cataloging-in-Publication Data

Tegarden, Diane 1957-
How to Escape a Bad Marriage- A Self Help Divorce Book for Women

ISBN 978-0-9745369-3-4

1. Self Help
2. Women's Issues
3. Relationships

This book can be ordered wholesale by libraries, battered women's shelters, women's organizations, and therapists by contacting the publisher.

Published by FireWalker Publications, Inc.
3579 E. Foothill Blvd. #322
Pasadena, CA 91107
Email: rosefirewalker@aol.com

Visit us on the web at www.firewalkerpublications.com

Cover Art Design by Delaine Ulmer

Printed in the United States by Lightning Source Inc.

ACKNOWLEDGEMENTS

Like a nervous new actor at the Academy Awards, I know I'll forget someone, so I apologize in advance if I omit any of my fabulous team members. My sincere thanks go to all the help given to me by the following people: my mother (Nina) and sister (Emily) for their encouragement to be myself and to keep on writing; my husband, for having a life and a mind of his own, and for not cramping my style; my wonderful, hard working publicist, Jackie O'Neal; my ever-patient graphic designer, Delaine Ulmer; Melissa Uribe from Melissa at the Spa, for being an awesome friend and supporter of this project; my brother, Phoenix, for being an honest and loving friend; the support staff at my printer's, Lightning Source Inc., Anne Pollock and Mary Gnetz, for their invaluable help putting the manuscript together; Reece Manley, a battered woman's counselor, for using this book to help more battered women escape the nightmare of domestic violence; Tony Robbins, for being an instrumental, life-changing force in my life; Marietta Henry, who walks her talk and has been a kind aunt-in-law; and Jeannette (McCahon) Church, for being one of my first real mentors.

I also want to thank the many writers and therapists who reviewed the book over the years, including: Maya Mahant, Mikaya Heart, Marinela Kotsina, Carole Cherry, Stephanie Watson, Jack Huber, Maria Andrade, Kathy Ferris, Marsha Walker, Julia Nizinski, Anne Dennison, and Beverly Mahone.

Introduction to How to Escape a Bad Marriage

As we move into the new decade, I feel compelled to pose the question "Is Marriage Still a Valid Institution?"

According to the last US Census 50% of marriages end in divorce, and, the likelihood of women becoming impoverished due to a bad divorce is over 60%! I define a bad divorce as one that you are unprepared for, whether it's financially or emotionally.

I wouldn't go to Vegas and gamble with those odds, so why do so many women still feel that the highest attainable goal in a relationship is marriage?

Financial security, emotional security and a stable environment for their children all play a role in this decision. But is it even simpler than that? Is the promise of "happily ever after" too tempting to pass up or is it the incredible peer pressure that women are expected to marry and raise children?

I think we are socialized to believe that we need the legal status of marriage, but with so many marriages failing, we need to realize there is a way out of a bad marriage that doesn't involve being homeless or impoverished.

With a bit of planning, financial savvy and forethought, we can prepare our pocketbooks and our children so that we can gain financial and emotional freedom from a bad marriage.

That's what this book is intended to do.

May it bring you the peace of mind that will lead to your freedom from a bad marriage,
Diane Tegarden
April 2010

How To Use This Book

Four Types of Divorce, Listed By Difficulty

In terms of emotional pain, no divorce is easy, but in terms of battles over material things, some are easier than others. First, we will outline several examples of divorce (not all scenarios will be included, but choose the one nearest yours and proceed). Then use only those sections of the book most helpful to your case.

Easiest Divorce

1 You don't jointly own any major items (major items are contracts you both signed to pay for something together).
2 You don't work together.
3 You don't have children together.
4 Neither of you is fighting the divorce.

See: Chapters 1, 3 & 7.

Fairly Easy

1 Each owns your own car, whether paid off or still paying off.
2 You don't work together.
3 You have kids, but there are no major arguments on child custody.
4 Neither of you is fighting the divorce.

See: Chapters 1, 3, 6, 7 & 9.

Harder

1 Each of you owns your own car, but you have signed together on a house, and neither cars nor house are paid for entirely.
2 You work together.
3 You have custody arguments/issues.
4 There are questions about what you own as individuals versus community property and possessions.
5 One or both are angry.

See: Chapters 1-4, 6-9.

Hardest

1 You both have signed on cars and a house, and nothing is paid for entirely.
2 You own a business together.
3 You have serious custody problems, or perhaps even child abuse issues.
4 One spouse is a batterer, physically violent and possessive.

See: Chapters 1-4, 5, 6-9.

Table of Contents

Chapter 1
Financial Independence

So you want to leave your spouse. You've thought about it many times. You have even daydreamed about freedom. Though you think you haven't a dime to your name, you still want to leave. Yet you find yourself worrying about leaving behind the material things that you do have.

Being in this state, when you can't go and you don't want to stay is called "LIMBO." Please understand that, regardless of your financial worth, being clear about your financial status will **EMPOWER** you, although you must put some work into it. You may choose to use your lack of understanding financial matters to prevent you from taking the next step, but if you truly want to leave, don't use this as an excuse not to go forward.

Often, women who are in this state of limbo focus on dealing with the emotional issues. To get yourself out of that mental place, it is more important to use this as a perfect time to educate yourself about the numbers.

Let's Begin to Figure It Out

Begin the process by taking stock of your **ASSETS**. Assets are items of value. They include: your house, rental property, pension plans, bank accounts, stocks, bonds, cars, businesses, antiques, life insurance, household furnishings, etc. You may be surprised while making this list to find out the actual value of what you own. When preparing this checklist, you should add any additional items you consider of value.

Please take time to ****Fill out the Assets Form NOW**** (all HIGHLIGHTED WORDS are defined in the Glossary at the back of the book).

Next, fill out the **Monthly Living Expenses/Budget Worksheet.** Your debts are commonly referred to as liabilities. These include: the mortgage on your house, monthly rent on your apartment, car loans, credit card debt, lines of credit, lease commitments and any other debts.

When you tackle this checklist, remember that these obligations will hold all parties liable for 100% of the debt. That means that if one of the parties doesn't make the payment, the other person will be held liable.

The sum of all of these items should be entered on the Total Monthly Living Expenses line of the form.

Now, put down your monthly net income from wages, add other income (including spousal or child support), and put the sum on the Total Income line.

Subtract your total monthly living EXPENSES from your INCOME, and you have either a net income (+) or a net loss (–) for the month. The result is either a positive number, meaning you have money to spare at the end of the month; or it is a negative number, meaning you will need to reduce your expenses to below the amount of your income. This is known as Budgeting!

Assets Form

Assets:

Cash in Checking Account:	+$_________
Cash in Savings:	+$_________
DIVIDENDS AND SECURITIES:	+$_________
CASH SURRENDER VALUE OF LIFE INSURANCE:	+$_________
Cash distributions from business:	+$_________
Value of Residences:	+$_________
Value of Vehicles:	+$_________
Retirement Plan Value:	+$_________
Other Assets:	+$_________
Other Income: Spousal Support/Alimony or Child Support:	+$_________
Total of all Assets	**+$_________**

Liabilities:

Mortgage and Notes Payable:	–$_________
Income Taxes Past Due:	–$_________
Other Liabilities:	–$_________
Total all Liabilities	**–$_________**
Take the total of all Assets and Subtract the total of all Liabilities	$_________
= YOUR NET WORTH (+/–)	**$_________**

Monthly Living Expenses/Budget Worksheet

TYPE OF EXPENSE	***Approx. Monthly Amount***
Mortgage or rent payments	$________
Real estate taxes	$________
Property insurance	$________
Electricity	$________
Natural gas	$________
Water/Sewer/Garbage	$________
Housing repairs, maintenance	$________
Telephone	$________
Yard Maintenance	$________
Food and household supplies	$________
Appliances and tools	$________
Vehicle: Loan/lease payments	$________
Insurance	$________
Repairs and maintenance	$________
Licensing fees	$________
Gasoline	$________
Medical costs/not insurance:	
Medication/prescription	$________
Health	$________
Psychiatric/psychological	$________
Dental-all	$________
Vision	$________

(Continued next page)

Monthly Living Expenses/Budget Worksheet (Cont'd.)

Health Insurance	$________
Life and Disability Insurance	$________
Toiletries and sundries	$________
Dining & Lunches out	$________
Clothing purchases/maintenance	$________
Educational costs: Tuition/books	$________
Beauty shop	$________
Club dues and membership fees	$________
Day care and baby-sitting	$________
Pet Care/Medical	$________
Sports/hobbies/camp	$________
Vacation	$________
Newspapers/Periodicals	$________
Professional Services (legal, accounting)	$________
Tax Payments: Income taxes	$________
Contributions	$________
Credit Card Payments	$________
Savings/Retirement/Investment	$________
A. Total Monthly Living Expenses	**$________**
Additions: Monthly Net Wages (Wages less taxes):	+$________
Other Income: Spousal Support/Alimony or Child Support	+$________
B. Total Income	**+$________**

NET MONTHLY INCOME=
Total Income (B.) *minus*
Total Monthly Living Expenses (A.) (+/–)$________

Budgeting Techniques

Sometimes, a discussion on finances can be a little overwhelming, so take some time to try and learn about each area individually.

Here are some important questions to ask yourself:

1. Do you know how much money it takes to run your household? Start keeping track of where your money is spent, this will establish your STANDARD OF LIVING and help you establish your budget. This includes keeping track of credit card charges and cash purchases.
2. Can you determine what changes you will need to make if you are on your own?

You will need to develop a realistic household budget, one that can support yourself and your children on your salary and any child support payments or assistance you may receive. Pretend you are on your own and think about how you alone would deal with the bills that will come your way.

By empowering yourself in the financial area, you can better understand your options. The biggest mistake you can make is to let events take their course while your watch helplessly from the sidelines, just because you didn't learn to deal with the numbers.

When getting a divorce, this process of understanding money is a reality you have to deal with. As cold as this may sound, think of the alternative. If you walk away with nothing, you and your children could suffer serious consequences – even become homeless. You need enough money to start over, and planning and preparation are your best tools.

Now that you have figured out your monthly budget, you may realize that most likely you'll need to reduce monthly expenses.

Here are a few areas to look at to make a monthly budget effective:

1. Consider reducing your monthly housing expense by sharing an apartment.
2. Be conscious of utility bills; turn off lights and appliances when not in use. Conserve water.
3. Set up direct deposit for your checking account; avoid a monthly service fee.
4. Join a credit union. This is especially useful when you need to borrow money at a lower rate and save at a higher rate than at a bank!
5. Pay off your credit cards. Cut them up and don't buy anything you don't absolutely need on credit again.
6. Ask if you can borrow money from your life insurance policy, in the event of an emergency.
7. Cancel all unnecessary periodicals, magazines and newspapers.
8. Be aware of your shopping habits; evaluate any spending that is not essential.
9. Don't pay full price for anything! Many stores and supermarkets sell name brand food and toiletries for half-price if you buy in bulk. It's worth the savings to clean out a hall closet and use it for the storage of extra paper products and dry goods, in order to buy in larger amounts. For example: Costco, Smart & Final, Sam's Club and other discount store prices are usually half what you pay in the grocery stores. While you can't get everything you need from the clubs, you can get a lot of name brand products for huge savings off your food bill.
10. When you feel like eating out, treat yourself to breakfast instead of dinner. It's the cheapest meal of the day. At some fast food restaurants, you may not have to tip, saving you 15% of the meal's cost. Take extra food home, so that you have part of your next meal prepared.
11. Comparison shop.
    a. Shop by telephone for the best purchase price on your big money items, like: appliances, electronic goodies, cars, etc. Talk it up among your co-workers and friends, if you plan to buy an expensive item. People like to share their horror stories and their

successes alike, and you may get some good tips on where to go and where not to go for your particular item. Magazines like *Consumer Reports* make it their business to test and compare hundreds of products every year for quality and price. A quick trip to the library will help you locate the issue you need to look up the information on the product that you plan to buy.

b. Play the competition against each other. Remember, the sales person wants to sell the item to you as much as you want to buy it, so quote their competitors price and don't be afraid to try to get them to lower their price. Sometimes this ploy works, but sometimes the price can't be changed by the sales person. If you think you have some bargaining power, you can ask to speak to a manager in charge who may have the ability to lower the price.

12. Recycling can save you money! Instead of buying wrapping paper for gifts, you can reuse the beautiful calendar pages from last year's calendar, or use the colorful comic section from your newspaper for children's gifts.
13. Instead of buying expensive art for your workspace, you can use free posters from travel agencies. They throw these away by the armful, and get them for free, so they are usually pretty good about donating these to your cause. What better scenery to look at on your work break, than to gaze at your next vacation spot?
14. Instead of buying flowers for gifts, trim your roses and arrange them in a second hand glass vase for a quick belated birthday present or any other occasion.
15. *(Warning, this subject may be considered controversial!)* Quit guilt holiday shopping. Christmas gifts bring on big debts and big guilt. Christmas is supposed to be a blessed time of year, but it often turns into a recurring financial nightmare for many families. Here are some money-saving suggestions:

    a. Instead of giving individual presents, which can set you back hundreds of dollars depending on the size of your extended family, have a family party. Everyone can bring a favorite food dish or sweets, share their funny and harrowing stories from the year gone past or maybe even sing together.

b. Help the children present a play to the rest of the family; each child could share a tale of the past year's adventures or a family anecdote that brings you together. This is the time of year to share a part of your life that your family may have missed or just to catch up on the latest family news. Instead of presents, adults might give each other IOU's for favors like baby-sitting, gardening, a massage, a facial, or share whatever your special hidden talent may be.

c. Some families draw names so that each family member exchanges one gift; this reduces the number of gifts needed by each family. Or, you can set a dollar limit on the amount of the gifts, to keep spending down to a dull roar. My #1 rule of Christmas finance: If you are still paying off last year's credit card debts due to Christmas shopping by the time the next Christmas rolls around, you are overspending!

16. Take advantage of the many free ways you can learn about finances. Local communities have free seminars put on by financial planners, attorneys, and accountants, to name a few. Go to as many of these as you like and take notes. You will be surrounded by other people who are there to learn, and you may begin to establish new business contacts.

17. Another place to check for financial information is your local library or community center that offers similar programs. Keep in mind that you're there to learn, not to buy. If you are approached by anyone selling products or services, just say, "I enjoyed your seminar and learned a lot, but I'm not interested in buying at this time." Do not give out your name, address or phone number on mailing lists, this way you won't be solicited at a later time. Financial education boils down to understanding the simple principles of addition and subtraction. You will be amazed at how everything can be **QUANTIFIED** in pluses or minuses.

18. Beware the "new clothes myth" that can ruin your budget. We know we can become obsessed with our wardrobe, buying matching clothes, shoes and purses with each new fashion and season. This is a colossal waste of money!

a. Remember, in any budget, clothes are considered a **DISPOSABLE EXPENSE,** because they can be used up in a year or less, while a car (maintained well) is considered an **INVESTED EXPENSE** because it can last up to ten years. In some cases, part of the expense for your car can be written-off your taxable income as a business expense. These are called employee reimbursable expenses, like maintenance and gas.

b. If you think that buying a new outfit will get you a raise, just look around at the company you work in. Chances are, the people at the top have about five good suits that they wear week in and week out, not hundreds of new clothes to impress the lower ranks. Their work, their degrees, their experience and their buddies (who they know), earn them their raises. Knowing how to make that money work for them is what helps to keep their money in their checkbook. Making less of your appearance, spending a sensible amount on clothes, make-up, bags, shoes and other accessories, makes your boss concentrate on your work, not your looks. This is how you will earn more.

c. If you must buy a new outfit, make it useful for several occasions, not just for work. Consider the money you will save, not to mention the environment, when you buy washable clothes instead of ones that need to be dry-cleaned!

d. Finally, if you have children, consider taking them to an up-scale third hand store. It will be a funky adventure for them to find their own wild outfits, saving you lots of money on clothes that will soon be outgrown anyway. This will give the kids some individuality in their wardrobe without making them feel poverty stricken.

My Tips on How to Get Out of Credit Card Debt

This is a method I have used and shared with many, many people, who have managed to dig themselves out of credit card debt in three years or less. This may seem like a long time, but many people, if left to their own financial devices, end up either in bankruptcy or in longer debt than the three years I propose.

First, make a list of all your credit cards, using columns for each of these items: name of card, the total amount.

Then, figure out how much you pay in credit card payments total per month.

Next, find the credit card you are closest to paying off with the highest interest rate. It is very important to understand that when you are buying items on credit you are paying more for them than the actual "sales" price, this is how the credit card companies make their money. Therefore, if you pay off this card first, you are automatically saving money by not paying a higher interest rate on the temporary loans that we call credit card debt.

It is critical to take the next few steps, even it is extremely painful. While trying to pay off a credit card, you must first cut it up and not use the account again until all your cards are paid off. Make a ceremony of it, and take a big old pair of scissors, while cackling with glee as you snip that debt into little unrecognizable pieces. It's exhilarating, try it, try it, I say!!

The next step out of credit card debt is to play the Money Shuffle.

The Money Shuffle

In the money shuffle, you take advantage of one of those wonderful special offers you're always receiving in the mail without asking for. Namely, a special offer for a credit card with a really low APR (3% or less), for a limited time only, usually six months. Fill out the application, and when they ask you about credit card transfers, transfer the total amount you pay per month on credit cards, multiplied by the number of months the special rate is in effect. Transfer this amount from the higher interest rate card to the new card. Make sure to pay it off completely within that time period, because after that the rates go up.

After you have paid off the card, cancel the card formally in writing, and keep a copy of your cancellation letter for yourself. In order to clean up your credit report and earn better interest rates and higher credit limits in the future, you must first get those bad debts off your record by paying them off. Then, once you actually cancel your account, your financial picture looks better to bankers and other people in your future.

One more note about the money shuffle that may surprise you. You may think, "it won't impress anyone to get a credit card and cancel it in six months." Oh, how wrong you are, my friend. In fact, paying off a debt on time is so very impressive that after you do this just once, more credit card companies will come calling at your door.

And I encourage you to avail yourself of another opportunity to play the money shuffle, to keep transferring your debts from a higher interest card to the lower one, eliminating the largest debt and establishing a new credit profile.

I suggest you immediately cut up all of the clothing store credit cards and specialty store credit cards. These usually have higher interest rates than other cards, and are for items that you should not buy unless you have the cash in your pocket. This method of deciding what to buy with credit cards can save you hundreds of dollars a year in disposable debts.

Basically, economizing means tightening your belt against the day you will have to support yourself and family. While you can't expect to continue living the lifestyle you're used to, you can learn to live on less without feeling IMPOVERISHED, if you learn the difference between DISPOSABLE EXPENSES (money you end up wasting) and INVESTED EXPENSES (money you can make count twice.)

The next part of the financial equation is to EARN MORE MONEY.

Earning More Money

One thing to consider is increasing your income by improving your saleable skills. If you attain a higher level of education, whether it's a certificate from a trade school, an AA or AS from a two-year college, or a BA or higher degree from a university, you will instantly be worth more money in the job market.

The question then becomes: Which school is right for you?

Trade School	**Two-Year College**	**Four-Year College**
Shortest time frame	Longer	Longest
8-12 months	3-4 Years	5-8 Years

If your main concern is on time, trade schools take the least amount of time, and usually have job placement available.

If your main concern is cost, and you have limited resources available, consider this: with your newfound financial independence, you will probably qualify for some type of financial aid, which is available at all three types of schools. Also, two-year colleges are very inexpensive and geared for returning students.

You will need to consider what type of job you are looking for and the educational requirements of the position you want. The chart below may help.

Trade Schools	Two-Year College	Four-Year College
Medical Assistant	LVN, RN	Doctor
Bookkeeper	Business Administrator	
Dental Assistant		Dentist
Legal Aid	Pre-Law	Lawyer
Sales Assistant	Sales Manager	Business Owner
CADD		Architect
Website Designer		
Computer Programmer	System Administrator	

Having graduated from both academic and trade schools, I have found the advantages and disadvantages of each. The advantages of a trade school are:

1. It takes a shorter period of time to complete the course work and to graduate or become certified.
2. There are various forms of financial assistance. Programs cost less for people at lower income levels.
3. They are flexible about working around a working adult's schedule.
4. Because trade schools offer a more limited curriculum than academic schools, they are usually more focused on the area of study the student is interested in; eliminating the problem of having to take classes that have absolutely no interest to the student.
5. Many trade schools have a placement office to help graduates get good entry-level jobs right out of school.

The one serious limitation I've found to trade schools is that you earn a certificate, not a degree, so if you are looking to get a job that requires a degree, you should consider an academic institution. Both junior colleges and universities are academic institutions that award various degrees, from an Associate to a Ph.D.

The main disadvantage of going to a university is that it takes a long time to go through a degree program, anywhere from 4 to 8 ½ years, depending on how many hours you have to work to support yourself and family. However, the advantage is that you can now qualify for the higher paying jobs that require a degree, (see chart above).

A word of warning: competition is fierce in the entry-level job market for people with a BA or BS. Make sure you get some on-the-job training in your chosen field before you graduate and go looking for a job. You'll be many steps ahead of the competition.

If you haven't been to school in over ten years and don't know where to start, community colleges often have classes designed for working adults who want to retrain for another career. These classes are designed to prepare you for the higher-level college coursework.

There are also free online classes available in these basics, to add to or increase your skills, and hopefully your wages down the road.

In the next few pages, we will use some goal setting forms in order to set up your academic plan in steps.

Let us start by brainstorming the problem.

Brainstorming Problems

BRAINSTORMING a problem is an activity in which you write down as many parts of the problem as you can think of. Write down all the obstacles that stand in your way, as fast as you can. Don't worry about being neat; just jot down the different aspects of the problem you want to solve. At this phase, don't worry about prioritizing the different parts, or try to come up with solutions just yet. You will prioritize them in the next step. Write down anything that comes to mind, no matter how silly, trite or ridiculous.

After you have left the list alone overnight, you can cross out the things that seem less important or less critical to solve right away.

Now, write down at least two possible solutions for each obstacle.

Stepping Stones Flow Chart

Once you have some solutions, write them in doable steps for each quarter of the next year using the Stepping Stones Flow Chart. I think that by looking at your progress every 3 months (or quarter), you can feel more of a sense of accomplishment than by checking your flow chart every month.

Remember to use the chart to see your progress and celebrate successes at every quarter ending. You don't have to be lavish, just take a moment to cross off the things you've done, and treat yourself to a quiet cup of congratulations.

Be flexible and realistic with your chart. Take into consideration the busier times of year and don't over schedule those months. Keep some space available for the longer projects, and the ones that will inevitably slop over into the next quarter.

Brainstorming Form – Financial Independence

Finances	Family/Children	Job/Career	Special Concerns

PROBLEMS:

SOLUTIONS:

Stepping Stones Flow Chart – Financial Independence

Beginning Now:

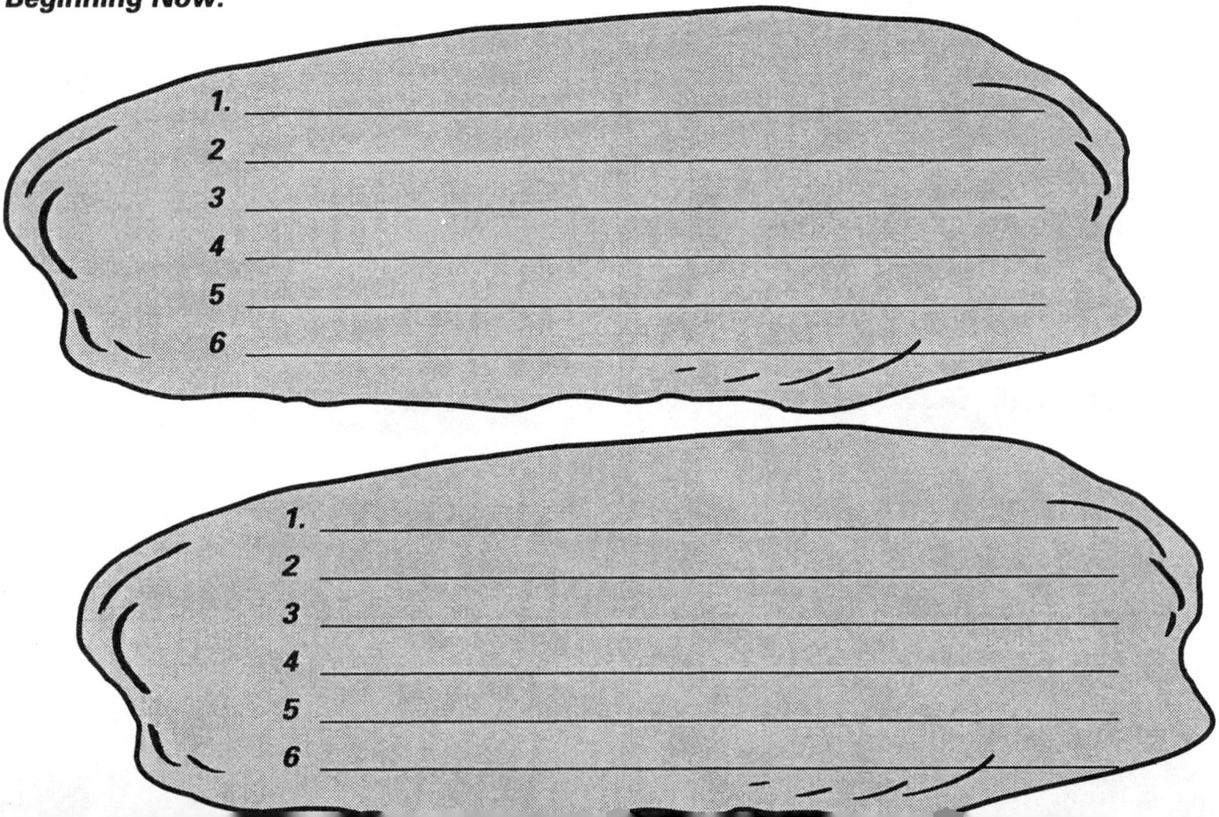

One Year Later!

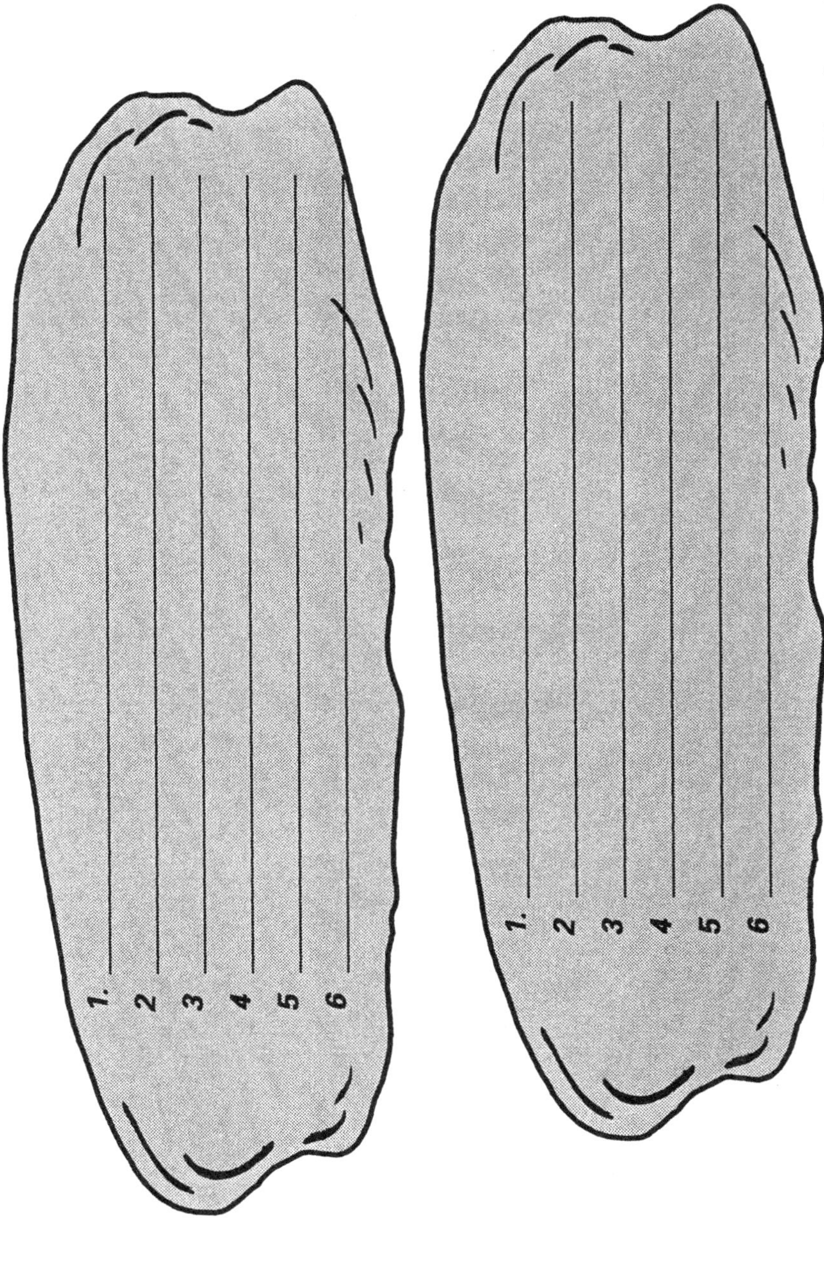

Chapter 2
Emotional Independence

Decisions, Decisions

In order to gain independence of any kind, you must first decide that you want to be EMOTIONALLY INDEPENDENT and then answer this question: "Is this relationship more good for me than it is bad?" Sometimes, it's hard to weigh each aspect of your situation, especially when your mind keeps bouncing from the good parts to the bad, from negative to positive like a ping-pong ball. To view your emotional relationship in a more visual way, let's take a look at the next form we will work with called "The Scale." It is designed to help you sort it all out.

Begin with the middle column "B" (representing all behaviors) and answer this question: "What are all the behaviors you particularly like *and* dislike about your spouse?" Do not worry about prioritizing them in any order or categorizing them just yet. Let your mind flow and scribble it all down. You can use the back of the page if you'd like, and basically write down everything that comes to mind.

I am a strong believer in letting your inner mind (or SUBCONSCIOUS) stew over large problems. After you make the list; set it aside for one night. The next day, scratch out all of the less serious offenses, and then put each remaining item in either column A (acceptable behaviors) or column C (unacceptable behaviors). If you really can't decide which column an item should go in, write it once in each column.

The Scale – Emotional Dependence

A Acceptable	B Behaviors/Actions	C Unacceptable

After you are finished, you'll have a visual representation of whether the relationship is more on the good side or more on the bad side. Usually, you'll see the scale tipping in one direction or another.

If column A has more items, your decision may be to stay in your relationship, or if you still wish to leave, you may be looking forward to a relatively easy divorce proceeding.

If both columns are equal, cross off the duplicate items in column A to see if the balance changes.

If column C has an overwhelming percent of the items, it may be time to make some permanent changes in your life.

Doctors Do Not Heal Themselves

After you decide you want to be emotionally independent, the next step is to get yourself some help in doing it! Women are taught from youth that the value in their existence is based on care giving. This idea can eat up your self-esteem.

Women are 100% complete people with or without a mate and with or without children. This is easier said than felt, however. To feel this from the inside, we have to be DEPROGRAMMED from thinking of ourselves only as "so-and-so's" wife or "so-and-so's" mommy. If we feel we cannot be whole people unless we regard ourselves in terms of our relationships with others, we cannot gain a healthy emotional independence.

We will go from one bad choice of spouse to another in order to maintain the image of ourselves that we have been taught, i.e., that we need someone to take care of in order to be important.

Who Should Help Us?

Believe it or not, professional therapists aren't that expensive anymore. For one thing, many insurance plans cover a certain amount for therapy. If you have medical coverage through work, call the plan administrator and ask if your plan covers therapy. If you don't have medical coverage, there are many clinics that work on a sliding scale. This means they charge you according to how much you make. Some charge as little as

$30.00 per session. Make some calls to see if local clinics have interns who work under the care of licensed therapists; they often charge a nominal fee. For a list of questions to ask when hiring the therapist, see the suggestions in *Chapter 4 -Using Professionals.*

People You Should Not Talk To

Most of the people you usually talk to about personal problems (parents, siblings, friends, or perhaps co-workers) either are in the same boat you are, or were raised with a lot of the social preconceptions that you were. While it may help to talk with them about your problems by venting emotions, they are of little help in convincing you to change your self-image.

That is why the person who is more likely to help you rebuild your self-esteem, will more than likely be a stranger. Sometimes you feel freer to change the way you act in front of someone who has no particular expectations of you. Did you ever notice, when you are with people you know, you fall into certain behavioral patterns when you're around them?

That's why professional therapists are a better choice to help you change yourself on a more permanent level.

Other People Who Are Involved

Of course, yours aren't the only feelings to take into consideration; your children and your spouse are also involved. Unless your spouse is violent or insanely possessive, you will need to talk to him and gauge his emotional state before you start to discuss who gets the furniture.

In order to get an idea about how your family is feeling, you can use the checklists on the following pages. Make a separate copy for each adult and each child age eight and up. Try to answer the questions as honestly as you can, in order to get an idea of how everyone is feeling about the dissolution of your family unit as it is now.

In-laws and "Out-laws"

Please note that I specifically did not include in the category of "Other People involved:" grandparents, in-laws, your siblings, your parents, or any other person.

Why? Because, no matter what anyone else thinks of your decision to get a divorce, only you, your ex and your children will have to live with that decision.

Many family members may lend you emotional support and help you out with the money, at first. But, eventually you and your ex will have to shoulder the financial and emotional responsibility for the decision.

A. Checklist for You:

How do you feel when you think about:	**A. You Want To Cry**	**B. You Feel Relieved**	**C. You Don't Care**
1. Sleeping alone every night			
2. Eating alone at restaurants			
3. Being a single parent			
4. Explaining your single status at work			
5. Explaining your single status to your family			
6. Explaining your single status to your kids			
7. Your ex with another woman			
8. You taking care of someone else's child			
9. Another woman taking care of your child			
10. Sharing custody of your children			

B. Checklist for Kids:

How do you feel when you think about:	A. You Want To Cry	B. You Feel Relieved	C. You Don't Care
1. Being from a "broken home"			
2. Explaining that you have only one parent to your friends			
3. Explaining that you only have one parent to your teachers			
4. Having to go back and forth from parent to parent			
5. Seeing your mom with another man			
6. Seeing your dad with another woman			
7. Sharing your parent with other children			
8. Having another "step" parent			

C. Checklist for Husband:

How do you feel when you think about:	A. You Want To Cry/ Get Angry	B. You Feel Relieved	C. You Don't Care
1. Sleeping alone every night			
2. Eating alone at restaurants			
3. Paying support for your children			
4. Explaining your single status at work			
5. Explaining your single status to your family			
6. Explaining your single status to your kids			
7. Your ex with another man			
8. Being a part time parent			
9. Another man taking care of your child			
10. Sharing custody of your children			

Difficult Child-Custody Decisions

Get ready for a shock. What if your children don't want to live with you?

This may be a blow to your ego and self -esteem, but the children may decide they want to stay with their father for whatever the reasons, whether it be financial or the fact that they are at "that age" when it's extremely "uncool" to live with your mom. They may decide to live with your ex, and you may find this impossibly hard to accept.

When a woman is not "awarded" custody of her children, she is often frowned upon in today's society in general, because it is still considered (primarily) the woman's responsibility to be the main childcare provider.

Unfortunately, since men generally earn more than women, and decisions are now being based on who can financially support a child, rather than who can better emotionally care for a child, some custody is being awarded to the father.

So, if this happens to you, you may suffer from wounded pride, ego, or low self-esteem. However, with work and patience, you can recover your poor financial standing and re-apply to gain full custody of your children.

Society expects the woman to be the primary childcare provider, homemaker and to do all this while working full-time. It is a heavy responsibility to take on all three at the same time, and women's health has greatly suffered for it in the last thirty years.

One way to solve this situation is to ease the burden on you. First, realize that you don't have to live up to anyone else's expectations of home making. Relax the perfect ideal of "keeping the perfect home" and being the "perfect mom."

Second, figure out ways to reduce the stress at work, if possible. Only you know your financial situation, but if you could get a similar job with equal pay and calmer working conditions, it may be worth the hassle of changing jobs.

Third, you can and should share childcare responsibilities with, your ex-husband, parents, other relatives, and friends who also have children.

As painful as it may be to admit to yourself, if your financial situation will not allow you to properly care for your children, you may need to let someone else care for them temporarily until you get on your feet financially.

All the encouragement in the world can't make you make the decision to divorce, only you can decide: if, when and how you will start your new life.

Chapter 3
Working Together Creates Special Problems

Should I Stay or Should I Go?

When you and your partner work for the same company, it can create all sorts of problems. First of all, you are "putting all your eggs in one basket" financially. This isn't good economics, especially considering all the downsizing and layoffs companies are going through right now. When your company goes through a layoff, if one of you gets laid off, the partner who is laid off may feel inferior or angry, and the one who remains may feel superior or guilty. This in itself can cause hard feelings between people, but these feelings can be worked out equitably.

Another problem arises when you both work together: at the end of the day, you don't have new experiences to share, and it becomes a huge complaint session that never ends, regarding your jobs. Both your complaints and successes become old hat, and you can grow bored with each other very quickly with nothing new to share.

If you do decide to separate and you're still working for the same company, your ex-spouse may be in a position to adversely affect your raises, promotions, even whether you can comfortably continue to work for the same company. The last thing you need is to be running into your ex-spouse in the hallway every day after you have gone through the trouble of a legal separation. You will not be emotionally free to go on with your life if you have to face your past every day.

The Emotional Impact of Working Together

Wisdom is buried in old clichés, especially the ones that remind us that: "Absence makes the heart grow fonder" and "Familiarity breeds contempt." Working with one's spouse can be very perilous.

Here is a laundry list of the various disadvantages of working together, followed with the solutions we have tried and whether or not the solutions worked.

Laundry list of disadvantages

#1. You're never "off" work because one or the other of you is usually talking about the business. It's harder to "leave the job behind" than you think!

#2. If it's a home based business, you are always reminded of "just one more thing to do" because it's right in the next room waiting for you. The workday turns out to be never ending.

#3. You don't have anything new to share because you've just spent the last 8–10 hours at the same place, and soon everything becomes "old hat."

#4. You can't take vacations from the boss because you're married to him.

#5. Often, more is expected of you than of other employees.

#6. Sometimes, depending on how the ownership of the business is set up, you don't receive the same benefits as regular full-time employees.

#7. You can become too business-like with your personal relationships or become too personal at work.

#8. If you're mad at your co-worker you may have no one else to talk to about it.

#9. If you have a serious disagreement at work it affects your home life considerably.

#10. It can become a serious struggle to have a truly EQUITABLE relationship (one with equal respect and decision making power), if your partner in business lords it over you at work all day.

#11. It's mentally and physically distracting to work together when you are still in the lovey-dovey stage, both for you and your co-workers.

#12. It's financially unsound, having "all your eggs in one basket" so to speak. In case of lay-offs at your company, you are risking 100% of your income.

#13. No matter how fair you try to be, other employees become suspicious of nepotism (special consideration because of a family tie).

#14. The other workers often feel outnumbered; the old "two-against-one" thinking prevails here.

The following sample case studies will illustrate these points by describing some scenarios and reviewing potential solutions.

Case Studies

SAMPLE CASE STUDY A:

Description: You and your spouse work together as fellow employees at the same company.
Level of Difficulty: This is the easiest to solve, once you answer these few questions.

Q. Which of you has seniority? Who has the greatest power to affect the other's position in the company?

A. If your spouse can cause you to be fired or demoted or to be miserable at your job every day, perhaps it would be best to get a new/better/ upgraded job to separate your income further from his. This should be done before you get divorced.

Q. How much money are you making?

A. If you are the major breadwinner in your household, you may have more leverage at your job than your husband. This is something only you can decide.

Q. What is it worth to you?

A. If your spouse can get you fired from your job, you may fight it as discrimination and win. But, what if you don't win? You're still out of a job and now you look bad to future employers.

The first case is the easiest because it is a finite question. If you are co-workers, the company will side with either the employee with more seniority (the one who has been there the longest) or the employee with the most power (most likely the higher wage earner). The facts are in front of you. Is he going to be able to affect your position in the company (get you fired or demoted)? Does he have a large number of cronies (friends at work) who could make it miserable for you every day after you had him fired? If you make a high-paying wage and have hiring and firing decision-making capabilities, you may choose to stay. Only you know what you have invested into the job. Will it be better to stay and tough it out with him around every day? Or will it be better to get your resume updated and look for a better job?

Disadvantages: 1/3/7/8/9/10/11/12/13/14

Solution to #1

Set a one hour time limit on the time at home you can spend talking about work. It's not easy. Often, one will start talking about something that had happened at work that day (whether exciting or exhausting), then the other will reply, and then you'll go back and forth, and so on. One hour ends up becoming three and your evening is gone. Try to set up a system of rewards if the time limit is honored.

Solution to #3

In order to avoid this trap, we tried to ban all work talk at home but that didn't work. We also set aside one night a week to play board games or some other interactive play, but truthfully the TV is rarely turned off on weeknights, and our scheduled date nights were often canceled.

I purchased several magazine subscriptions to keep a variety of reading materials in the house that were non-work related. Instead my spouse insisted on bringing home trade manuals to read on the weekends. Needless to say, I wasn't the least bit interested in talking about those publications.

Solution to #7

Try to work in different departments, or even different branch offices of the same company, to separate your personal vs. professional relationship. At least if you each have different work environments, you'll have different experiences, co-workers, duties, and individual accomplishments to share at the end of the day.

Solution to #8

Unfortunately, if you get into an argument at work about work with your spouse, you don't have anyone to talk to about it.

Suggestions:

A. Develop a network of good listeners to rant and rave to.
B. Try physical activity to help relieve the anger.
C. Seek the help of a relationship MEDIATOR/therapist to learn how to talk to your mate about these disagreements.

Solution to #9

If you can't solve the problem at work that caused the argument, it will more than likely follow you home. We tried ignoring the problem once we'd get home, but it seemed to resurface until the actual problem at work was solved.

Solution to #10

I have always felt that women and men are equally important and equally valuable. However, society sometimes places women in a position of secondary or lesser importance than men. In my struggle to attain equal status with men, I have found economic equality (making close to or the same amount of money) is a great way to level the playing field. I have seen many examples of this in action with women who have worked in the home (non-paid labor), then gone out and gotten jobs outside the home. Immediately, their sense of self-worth begins to develop, and they begin to feel and think more as individuals. Once they earn more they feel they have a proprietary right to decide how the money is spent.

In the world of men, power and respect don't necessarily equal strength, but often, strength is represented by the size of one's salary. Therefore, in order to gain a more equal relationship with your mate, you must equal his money-making abilities (or nearly equal). This brings more personal power and respect to you both at work and at home.

Solution to #11

It is unprofessional to snuggle with your mate in front of your co-workers, so be affectionate at home, not the office. At work, call each other by first names, not pet names.

Solution to #12

Obviously, working for two different companies is the better way to go.

Solutions to #13 & #14

It's difficult to shake the accusation of favoritism and nepotism once they become rooted in the minds of your co-workers. The best way to avoid these accusations is to set standard policies of conduct, job performance, rewards and discipline; to assure every employee is treated the same. You will also find documentation a critical part of proving equal treatment among all employees.

SAMPLE CASE STUDY B:

Description: You are married and work out of your home or own a small business, often referred to as a "Mom and Pop Shop."
Level of Difficulty: This has an advantage, in that, if you live in a community property state (Arizona, California, Idaho, Louisiana, Nevada, New Mexico, Texas, Washington and Wisconsin), you own half of the assets

and half of the bills of that business. So, depending on how prosperous or in debt the business is, you can sell your interest in the business back to him. This does not affect the amount of child support you will receive.

Mom & Pop Shops

As much as I have come to hate the phrase "mom & pop shop," it does correctly paint a picture of a family owned business. When you are a husband and wife team, business becomes "up close and personal" because you (as a couple) are 100% personally financially responsible for the debts of the business. This means that if you are married, and either you or your spouse is named as the sole **PROPRIETOR**, you are both personally responsible for all the debts of the business as well as your own personal debts! This also holds true if you and your husband are named partners in the business.

One way to separate your personal and business debts is to incorporate your business (the advantages are explained in Case Study C, so we'll leave the "why" and "how" details for later).

Disadvantages: 2/4/5/6

Solution to #2

Suffice it to say, besides many of the previously mentioned disadvantages, if it's a home-based business, you are always reminded of "just one more thing to do" because it's right in the next room waiting for you.

Yes, you can designate one room for a home-based business (if the business doesn't involve manufacturing or retail), but you still know it's there. Even if you can't hear that phone ring, you know work is always waiting to be done just beyond that door. (Hint: after work hours, you can turn off the ringer for that line.)

The problem setting so many restrictions on your new fledging business is that you may smother it to death. You may find, especially in the first three years, that many personal sacrifices are necessary in order to get it off the ground. It's like having a puppy in the house; it means long hours, it's noisy and messy, but it's worth the time once it's trained and able to get along on its own for a few hours!

Solution to #4

Suggestions:

1. Regular vacations! Just drag him away and once he's out there, he'll enjoy it.
2. Keep work contacts to a minimum once you do get away.
3. Working vacations (Seminars). This is an acceptable compromise, because you can go to school during the day and party at night. Stay the weekend and enjoy the city together. Remember to pick a beautiful place, one you've always wanted to see! If you own the business, you can write off most of the expense for the trip.

Solution to #5

More is expected of you than other employees. Many people suffer the false impression that if you own your own business, you can work only when you want to. They think that you enjoy short days, short weeks, long weekends, come in late and go home early. Nothing could be further from the truth! In point of fact, it is quite the opposite.

Many a start-up business began as a part time job, which supplemented the Nine-to-Five job. Eventually you can "quit your day job," but it can take up to three years before you can go solo. Then the fun really starts, as a 24/7/365 cycle of work that slowly eats up your time. Beginning in the morning: preparing to go to work, organizing work crews, picking up supplies, doing errands at noon, talking about your work day just past and planning for the up coming work day tomorrow. Help! Someone fire me please.

Over the course of a sixteen year relationship, (personal and working together), I have been expected to do what is necessary to get through each and every working day, including: receptionist, bookkeeper, taxes, web design, office manager, shipper/receiver, writer, editor, public relations, teacher, trainer and retail salesperson.

The only solution to being taken advantage of in this way, is to decide exactly what you will and won't do, (delineate the duties of your position) and stick to your guns. What happens when you don't draw the line? What happens when you wait too long?

Solution to #6

WAITING TOO LONG TO DRAW THE LINE

Q: What didn't they tell you about the straw that broke the camel's back?
A: The straw weighed 533 pounds!

I was at work one May afternoon when a shipment of three 100-lb. packages arrived. No one else was there, so the truck driver and I had to unload them, which was a strain on my back. However, ten minutes later a 16-wheeler came rolling in with the real shipment for the day; a 533 lb. one piece package of solar panels, all shrink-wrapped together in one long unwieldy package. The trucker and I had to get this bad boy off the truck, the bed of which is 6 feet high and well over my head.

We had a manually operated hydraulic lift, which I held while the deliveryman loaded the pallet onto it with a pallet lifter. Unfortunately, the load shifted as he set it down on the manual lift I was holding. It torqued my body, causing a rib to fracture and the ligaments in my sternum to tear. I was in excruciating pain for a week before I realized something was seriously wrong, and I went to the doctor. They took x-rays, and told me I was disabled and not to return to work for a month.

Unfortunately, the worker's compensation insurance we had would not cover my claim, because I was one of the business owners and therefore exempted from coverage. However, once you incorporate, you become an employee of the company, with the same workers' compensation benefits.

Moving On

When you are finally ready to go onto your new job opportunity, don't worry about training your replacement. What I mean by this is, don't fall for one of the oldest traps women fall for: "The company will fall apart without you here," "No one else can be trusted," "No one else cares like you do," etc. Some of the objections have a small basis in truth; however, it isn't healthy to believe that you are the only competent person in the world to do your job.

First of all, everyone in a company can be replaced, from the owners down to the contract laborers. The company will continue without you, although it may be a little bit tough at first. There are many capable people who can do your job, and yes, they may be less personally concerned with the company, but they can be trusted to do an adequate job. These objections to your leaving are based on fear, rather than information. If you can show your spouse that you have researched your replacements' qualifications, this should suffice.

To believe that no one will do what you do for your salary is probably true. Think about it. Your spouse may expect you to do your job, pick up the cleaning, keep the office running smoothly, go to the bank and post office, purchase office supplies, clean the coffee machine and run interference for him on the phone. Who would be expected to do two or three jobs and get paid for only one?

SAMPLE CASE STUDY C

If you work as business partners, it is absolutely critical to know the differences between a sole proprietorship, partnership and a corporation.

The sole proprietorship gives him a higher percentage of ownership or interest in the business, even if you both started it from scratch together.

If you are seriously thinking about setting up a business with a spouse, insist on a partnership, instead of a sole proprietorship. You will then be officially listed as an owner (this makes a difference later on), and you can take a stand with the strength of some authority when dealing with clients or other business associates.

Make sure you discuss these issues with your future business partner, so he is warned that you will work together only if there is an understanding that both your positions are equally important and are to be equally respected.

By being a named partner, you will also be able to sign official documents and receive the financial information you need to work with, without having to run to your spouse for a signature.

As far as LIABILITY issues are concerned; whether you are a partner in a business or the spouse of a sole proprietor (and working for him), the outcome is still the same.

If someone sues your company and wins, they can take away your house, cars and any other personal property to fulfill the debt. But, if you are a corporation, most of the time, your personal assets can't be taken in the settlement.

A corporate structure for your company protects your personal assets from lawsuits. If you both privately own 100% of a corporation, your personal property cannot be sold to pay for the company debts.

SAMPLE CASE STUDY D

If you are not married and are living together, you must take special care to guard your rights. If you are living together with a self-employed man, you have NO RIGHTS OF OWNERSHIP, even if you helped him build the business from scratch. You are not legally entitled to half the business assets, unless you are named as a limited partner. Be careful, you can work your tail off for free and not be compensated for it later if you two break up.

Chapter 4
Using Professional Help

Look Who's Talking!

When you're having hard times in a relationship, it can be confusing and frustrating. Many times, you may feel like pouring out your heart to someone, but it's best to be careful choosing whom to talk with about your personal problems.

WHOM NOT TO TALK TO:

Co-workers – ***DON'T!***
Family – ***DON'T!***
Friends – ***DON'T*** over do it, using them as an emotional washcloth!

Let's start with my suggestions about "who not to talk to," and how they got there.

CO-WORKERS

Friends at work are cool, but have you ever noticed how, once you've told your pal about the last argument you had with your husband, you feel silly once you see your friend again? Once they have taken your side in an argument, it's hard to get them to forget it and to "forgive" your mate! It can also be socially awkward the next time your friend and your spouse meet.

The other side of the coin is that, if you and your co-worker have an argument, they can emotionally blackmail you. Because they know about your personal problems, they can tell other co-workers, or worse yet, they may tell your boss! It reflects poorly on you all the way around, if co-workers know too much about your personal life.

FAMILY

Most of the time, complaining to your family about your choice of spouse is like throwing a boomerang. It'll come right back to hurt you right where you live. You want to avoid the "I told you so" looks, the pitying glances or the inevitable gossip that will start when your family finds out your desire to change your marital status. Again, it becomes socially uncomfortable when, at family gatherings, people may harbor ill will toward your partner for arguments that are long past. Of course, if you happen to be blessed with a non-judgmental family member, you may want to find comfort in their advice.

FRIENDS

You may ask, if I can't talk to friends, then what are friends for? You may feel they are there to listen to your innermost secrets, fears, and troubles; someone who is always on your side. I couldn't agree more. Friends can be sympathetic listeners and the keeper of the "skeletons in your closet," but let me also warn you: DON'T OVER DO IT!!

If every time you call your best friend, it's to complain about your spouse, it can become repetitious.

If you continually forget to ask your friend, "Is this a good time to talk?," you may become overwhelming for them to deal with. Friendship should be two-sided; they have their troubles, bad days, problems and secrets too. Remember to be considerate of their life. Don't just use them as an emotional washcloth.

INSTEAD TALK TO PROFESSIONALS/THERAPISTS

If you have co-dependency issues, are drug addicted, or are dealing with an abusive partner, you may need a professional therapist to help you understand how and why your situation came about, and how to cope with various tough decisions and choices.

I believe that up to a certain point, therapy is very helpful. Sometimes, if you understand why you behave a certain way, you can help yourself change from the inside out. You do have to invest a certain amount of time and money into it. Often employer paid health policies will include benefits for mental health. If you don't have health insurance, there are clinics that take patients on a sliding scale, (meaning they charge according to your income level). These clinics offer good care at reasonable costs.

A FINAL WORD ABOUT THERAPY

I've been to several therapists, and like any other professional who is giving you a personalized service, you two will have to "click." There are different schools of therapy, different approaches and, of course, individual styles of therapy, what people used to call a doctor's "bedside manner." You need to meet and try different therapists to see whose style and what method works best for you.

FREE THERAPY!

Free group therapy is sometimes available, for example: AA (Alcoholics Anonymous) and all their other affiliates. The meetings work extraordinarily well for some people. These groups are generally supportive, sympathetic and non-judgmental. The only requirement is that you approach your problems with a focus on the drug addiction in your life.

Lastly, in all seriousness, if you just want to get emotional garbage off your chest without repercussions coming back to haunt you, go to a bar and blab to strangers! (Just never go back!)

STRANGERS – A GOOD IDEA ACTUALLY!

Consider talking less serious problems out with: Waitresses, Hair stylist, Esthetician, Bartenders, Manicurists. These are the professionals in personal service jobs who are used to getting emotionally dumped on, so go ahead and get your problems off your chest, then leave them behind!

Sometimes it's intimidating to talk to high-powered (sometimes expensive) professionals like therapists, attorneys, or CPAs. Following are three checklists of questions you can ask, so you can come away from a phone call or interview with the information you need.

Checklist of Questions for Attorneys

These are questions you should ask before you hire an attorney:

1. Is the first consultation free (what will it cost)? ____________

2. What is your hourly rate for work?____________________

3. What is your retainer fee and what does this cover? __________

   ____

   ____

4. What documents do I need to have all the correct information available? ______________________________________

   ____

   ____

5. What percentage of cases do you settle as opposed to going to trial?

   ____

6. Approximately how long will it take to finalize?____________

   ____

7. Should I / can I move out of the house before the settlement?

   ____

8. Will we need an ACTUARY or forensic accountant? ____________

   ____

Checklist of Questions for CPAs

These are questions you should ask before you hire a CPA:

1. Is the first consultation free, or is there a fee?________________

   ____

2. What is your hourly rate for work?______________________

3. What is your entire fee and what does this cover? ____________

   ____

   ____

4. What documents do I need to have all the correct information available? ______________________________________

   ____

   ____

5. How long will it take to get the finished documents back?

   ____

Checklist of Questions for Therapists

Sometimes, an agency will need to interview you before they either accept you as a patient or before they will tell you their rates.

Questions you may be asked in an intake interview:

1. Why are you considering therapy? ____________________

____

____

2. Have you ever had therapy before? ____________________

____

____

3. If so, why aren't you continuing with that therapist? __________

____

____

4. Have you ever had problems with alcohol or drugs? __________

____

____

5. What is your marital status?________________________

The therapist then offers to treat you for a set amount per hour. You should ask about the types of counseling available, their rates per hour and the days and hours available for treatment.

Website Reference List

Here is a brief list of online resources, offering a range of divorce services.

www.nolo.com

Free legal advice in all areas of law, including: marriage, divorce, custody issues, wills & estate planning, small business and employment law, to name a few. This site also features a list of links to referral services for attorneys and offers a large selection of books on all facets of divorce.

www.divorcesource.com

This website offers information arranged in categories, such as: Finding Professionals, Children & Divorce, Divorce, Dollars and Debt, Surviving Divorce, etc. They have links to divorce professionals, books, record keeping information, and forms to use. Most of the links I followed lead to product pages where you can purchase divorce products online.

THERAPY ONLINE:

http://mentalhelp.net/psyhelp/chap10/chap10n.htm

The website is designed to give you general information about the emotional and mental aspects of divorce.

Chapter 5
Leaving a Battering Spouse

Whether we want to face the ugly truth about "domestic" violence (that it is an epidemic killing more women in this country than breast cancer), the fact remains that for whatever reasons, this is the hardest relationship from which to DIVEST yourself.

Research has shown that the abuser is usually a charming type of person, jovial and very attentive to details. He also waits to show his violent side until the woman is well into the relationship, either engaged or already married to him before she "finds out his ugly little secret."

The victim of abuse may also have an enabling type personality (see chart below for THE **ENABLER**), and may think that the abuser cannot live without her, trapping her in the cycle.

This disease (violence toward your mate is a disease) can rarely be cured, so once the abuser is rejected by his current victim, it doesn't take them long to find the next victim.

Divorcing violent abusers is extremely dangerous (just ask the family of Nicole Simpson-Brown, who was divorced from O.J. Simpson at the time of her murder). She had a restraining order on him at the time of her murder. What many good people don't understand, is that having a judge put a T.R.O. (Temporary Restraining Order) on a person will only protect you from law abiding people, not a violent spouse-abuser.

In order to grasp the seriousness of the situation, I will share a true story with you, putting you right in the middle of the nightmare.

The Last Night

Excerpt from *Forty-Five Days to Freedom* by Diane Tegarden

He was passed out drunk on the floor; his body sprawled in an unnatural position, my car keys clutched tightly in his left hand. I had already decided, the next time he drank until he blacked out I would leave him, I would gather the courage to take the car and leave him with only what I could carry.

But I left with even less than that.

As I gently tried to open his hand without waking him, he stirred in his sleep. I ran out then, leaving the door open behind me, terrified that he would wake up. I knew he would beat me "until I didn't move" as he had done before. Only this time, I knew he wouldn't stop.

I ran down the street. The tears in my eyes were making it hard to see, as I cried in fear and pain. I knew I could not go back to face his fists and towering rage. My hands shook as I put change into a public phone.

I called Haven House, a battered women's shelter I had heard about. I prayed fervently that they could house me until I recovered from the last six months of this living hell I had found myself in.

I decided to leave and never look back, because he had bragged that he had "killed the last bitch who dared to walk away" from his abuse. Once I found out they had a bed available, I thumbed a ride there.

Arriving alone and tired, I had to have an intake interview to make sure I qualified as a resident. Every shelter is funded differently and has different requirements for their residents, and fortunately, I was able to stay for their 45-day residential program.

For the first few days, you are not allowed to make phone calls to anyone you know outside the shelter. This is to insulate you from those people who may try to convince you to return to the batterer. The first twenty-four hours are the toughest, because you are recovering from the immediate pain of the beating, and you find yourself among strangers, without your familiar belongings and friends who usually help you through.

Since therapy is the most important tool in your recovery, you go to sessions all day long. First, a personal counselor will get the story of how you became involved in the abusive relationship, to get a clearer understanding of how the problem started. Then you go to group therapy to show you there are other people who have lived the same way you did.

Many times, living in an abusive relationship keeps you isolated from other people. The isolation is one of the tools he uses to keep you there. What causes you to stay? You figure everyone else has a decent relationship, that they work out these problems. You blame yourself for not being able to function in a decent relationship.

You figure if you try harder, if you love him more, if you compromise more, he will come around. Always, you blame yourself for any problems and keep them to yourself.

The shelters are so full that you have to room with another family in the cottage you are staying in. This works well, because once you open up and share the story of your abuse, you often realize that you are not the only person who has subjected herself to this degradation. And sometimes, when you hear the horror stories of other women, you may actually feel lucky to have escaped with your own injuries.

The woman and her five-year old son who shared my cottage went through unbelievable torture at the hands of her husband, a widely respected, conservative businessman. The last beating involved her being strangled with a bed sheet, then he dragged her to the bathroom by the neck and started banging her head on the sink. He then poured liquid drain opener on her head and was about to light the sheet when the police broke down her front door. The five-year old watched the whole scene in mute terror.

Two weeks later, when I met her, her raw bruises and burnt skin attested to his hatred. Her five-year old did not speak or play as any other child would, but hesitantly watched strangers for any quick movement, which would send him screaming from the room.

Needless to say, the staff is almost all women, but occasionally a male worker was on the property. The way these battered children would eye men in fear, like young colts ready to bolt, was simply the saddest thing to see.

They tell you that you should not go back to your old job because this is one of the first places he will look for you. And you must take your kids out of the school they usually attend, for the same reason. You cannot visit friends or family, because he will be looking for you in all your familiar haunts.

This means, along with getting your head into the right place, i.e., understanding that this behavior is not acceptable to you, you must learn how to support yourself and your children, find housing and manage not to get found, all in forty-five days!

Some women return to their husband after they stay at a shelter, because the prospect of taking care of themselves and their children is overwhelming. Some cannot stand the thought of losing everything that they have worked so hard to get, their house, their career or their children's education. The problem is, that if they remain in the relationship, they may not live to see their children go through school.

Look Inside for the Answers

It is always a difficult decision, but, once you have decided to leave, there are a few things you can do to prepare for this major life change. Start building a network of friends sympathetic to your situation, people who do not know your batterer, and are outside the home environment. It is surprising to find out that people will rally to help out, if they know the seriousness of the situation.

At work or school or in your community, there may be a support group for victims of spousal abuse. But don't introduce these people to the abuser, because if they can help you in safety, they may be more willing to help.

Do not discuss any plans to leave with your family or friends who may tell the abuser. This will only infuriate him and cause him to watch you more carefully.

However, you must have a plan in order for you to escape with life and limb, as well as your children and some possessions intact.

Why Some Women Stay Too Long

It makes me so angry when I hear a complete stranger to the situation blithely say, "Why doesn't she just leave him?"

The question assumes that:

#1. It is an easy thing to get a divorce, particularly from a violent, jealous person who doesn't want to let you go.

#2. You are healthy enough, mentally and physically, to move out of your home (if it became necessary).

#3. You have the financial resources to support yourself and your children, now.

#4. Your children want to leave the situation and are being co-operative.

These assumptions show a cold lack of compassion for the victim, an unbelievable ignorance of the cycle of "domestic violence" and a complete misunderstanding of how a person can become entrapped in such a situation. Not all women leave their spouses in time.

And not all women who stay too long are battered women. There are many other reasons why we stay too long, including:

1. Staying out of a sense of duty ("till death us do part").
2. Staying out of pity or guilt (you believe the person is so dependent on you that he will "die" without you).
3. Staying because your religion says it is wrong to be divorced.
4. Staying because your family believes "you have made your bed, now you must lie in it."

Some women want to stay until "you get even with him," because they want to "even the score" for his cheating, theft, or lies, to try to get the money back they've invested in him over the years.

It's true, the longer you stay in a relationship, the harder it is to leave. Whether out of a misplaced sense of duty to your spouse, family, church, or out of guilt and pity, only you can decide when you've paid the price for your beliefs. It will never be fair that you gave him the best years of your life, health, love and support, but you can't get those years back. The bottom line is, the longer you stay, the more you have to lose emotionally. However, you needn't fear poverty. You may need to make some lifestyle adjustments, but that won't be as hard as you may think.

A deeper fear (at least one of them), is that you'll end up a "lonely old woman who lives with eight cats." Again, society pressures us into thinking that it is a "curse" to be a woman who lives alone. Chances are, if you have developed a full life, you already have family, friends, co-workers, children, and business acquaintances. You'll be fine. Don't believe for a moment that just because you're divorced, you are suddenly "alone."

Learn To Recognize The Enemy

At this point you may be asking yourself, "How do I know if my partner is an abuser?"

The answer is not a simple one. It requires asking several questions about your prospective or current partner. Some of the symptoms of a batterer are: unfounded, intense jealousy; alcoholism (85% of domestic violence occurs while the batterer is under the influence); house beating (violence with household objects); history of being brought up in a violent home (60% of all U.S. couples engage in spousal abuse, and a violent home is where batterer's learn the abuse); any premarital slaps or hitting; a history of mental illness; aggression; perfectionism (doesn't admit to being in the wrong or making mistakes); charming; manipulative; blaming; any previous history of violence.

Unfortunately, battering comes in all colors and sizes. In other words people of all races, economic backgrounds, religions, ages and education levels can become batterers. They may be physically, sexually, mentally or emotionally abusive to you. It is up to you to determine what, if any, type of abuse is acceptable to you. But first, you must recognize that it is happening, without all the excuses you usually reserve for others as an explanation of your injuries.

DEALING WITH PHYSICAL ABUSE

Ask yourself if your intimate partner has ever done any of these things to you:

- pushed or shoved you;
- physically restrained you to keep you from leaving;
- slapped, bitten, kicked or choked you;
- hit or punched you;
- thrown objects at you or threatened you with a weapon;
- locked you out of your house or abandoned you in a dangerous place alone;
- refused to help you when you were sick, injured or pregnant; or
- subjected you to reckless driving or kept you from driving your car

Keep in mind, no matter how trivial the physical violence is at the beginning, it quickly escalates to dangerous and more serious violence against you. If you accept a certain level of abuse, this gives the abuser permission to continue the cycle, which most often ends in the death of the victim. In 1979, 40% of female homicide victims were killed by their domestic partner.

SEXUAL ABUSE

Sexual abuse is even harder to define, since the premise is that two consenting adults in a marriage have the right to and can expect to enjoy each other's sexual privileges.

The line between what is acceptable for intimate partners to do with one another and what is abuse, is a rather flexible one that changes with our own sexual needs. You might be fulfilling your partner's fantasies in bed, because he will do the same for you.

However, if you're doing something that makes you feel demeaned, or because you are afraid not to, or because you fear retaliation, you may want to examine the relationship closely. Being raped by your spouse is just as terrifying as being raped by a stranger.

MENTAL ABUSE

If you often wonder whether you're going crazy and begin to doubt your own judgment, you may be on your way to the mental state of mind that allows the abuse to continue. You become depressed and feel as if you'll never find a way out of your bad relationship.

Some sure signs of a batterer are: his ability to isolate you from your family or friends; creating emotional and financial dependency; minimizing the violence when it happens; denial that it happens at all; behavior that becomes more severe over time; trying to control all the money you make; threats to hurt you or your children; insane unfounded jealousy that you are having sexual relations with other men.

The list could be endless, but the question is, if these symptoms continue to worsen, how long will you stand for the abuse? You need to decide what is acceptable and what is not acceptable behavior from a partner.

Making A Choice About Your Abuser

In order to decide on what is acceptable behavior, and what goes over the line, use the next form, called THE SCALE.

First, write down all his behaviors; good, bad, large and small, important and trivial. Again, don't worry about prioritizing or organizing your responses. Put all the behaviors in the middle column. Then separate the behaviors into either the Acceptable or Unacceptable columns.

When you are through, you will have a clearly visible picture of your situation. This may help you to make the decision to end the abuse and leave him.

But before we go on to the planning stages of your departure, let's go over some more key information on spousal abuse and alcoholism.

Alcoholism and its cycle of co-dependency are one of the number one factors common in both the abuser and the abused. The entire family becomes involved in living the life of dependency with the alcoholic. Every family member is affected, and each reacts within the patterns of co-dependency.

The following information explains the dynamics of living with alcoholism, and how it affects your family.

The Scale – Making a Choice About Your Abuser

A Acceptable	B Behaviors/Actions	C Unacceptable

Some Facts About Alcoholism and Domestic Violence

Information provided by: Haven House
P. 0. Box 50007, Pasadena, CA 91115-0007 – (213) 681-2626

The National Council on Alcoholism has defined alcoholism as *"a chronic, progressive and potentially fatal disease."* It is characterized by tolerance, physical dependency and/or pathological organ changes; all are the direct or indirect consequences of the alcohol ingested.

- It is estimated that approximately 100 million Americans drink.
- Of that number, there are approximately 10 million adult Americans who have developed the disease of alcoholism and 26,000,000 with potential problems with alcohol.
- For every person with alcoholism, at least five other lives are negatively affected, primarily family members living with the alcoholic.
- Fifty percent (50%) of the children living in alcoholic homes will develop alcoholism (this figure is significantly increased if both parents are alcoholics).
- It has been estimated that about forty percent (40%) of the children living in alcoholic homes will marry alcoholics. This happens because children only learn to live in a home filled with alcoholism.
- Estimates of how many child abusers are alcoholics range as high as 60%. More than 1/4 of incest cases are alcohol related.
- In their efforts to compensate for and cope with the alcoholic, the family progresses through the stages of the disease in the same manner as the person with alcoholism and ultimately may reach the same three choices: death, insanity or recovery.
- Alcohol related deaths might run as high as 205,000 per year, including up to 10,000 injuries and up to ½ of all homicides.

Some Characteristics of The Batterer and His Families

From: *The Responsibility Trap,* by Claudia Bepko and Jo Ann Krestan.

In a family where there is this type of stress, every member changes and shifts behavior patterns to try to bring balance, stability, and survival. This is the type of dynamic each of us entered into when we came into a family.

In a chemically dependent family, each of these individual parts is affected by the growing dysfunction of the chemically dependent person. Each family member adapts to the behavior that causes the least amount of personal stress. Just as the chemically dependent person is suffering from self-delusion in regard to the use of the chemical, so are the family members self-deluded. As the chemical disease progresses, each family member compulsively represses his/her feelings and learns to react with a survival behavior. This behavior serves to build a wall of defenses for protection from pain.

As the CHEMICALLY DEPENDENT PERSON goes through the progression of the illness, the feelings of guilt, shame and fear grow. They must be hidden under outside behavior that con-vinces others that "every-thing is fine."

The CHIEF ENABLER is the person who is the closest and the most depended on by the dependent. The Enabler becomes totally involved in the mood swing of the dependent. To keep the semblance of normalcy, the Enabler needs to become more and more responsible.

The FAMILY HERO can see and hear more of what is happening in the family and begins to feel responsible for the family's pain. The hero works hard to make things better for the family and works diligently to improve the situation.

The SCAPEGOAT does not wish to work so hard to prove himself worthy. The Scapegoat looks for others for peer support.

The LOST CHILD suffers loneliness even though being alone is the situation where there is most com-fort for that child. The growing chaos of the family pressures the LOST CHILD to look for validation within personal resources, such as fantasies.

MASCOTS are often cute, fun to be around, and able to use charm and humor to survive in a painful family system. No one sees the fear and insecurity deep within the Mascot.

Alcoholism and the Family / Self-Worth and Needs

ROLE	BEHAVIORS	SELF WORTH	NEEDS
CHEMICALLY DEPENDENT PERSON	grandiose aggressive guilt righteous no mistakes charming blaming	shame inadequacy accountability loved accepted	confrontation support
THE CHIEF ENABLER	super responsible puts others first fragile sickly powerless compliant manipulative	anger guilt tired expression of feeling	support self care confrontation
THE FAMILY HERO	successful performs well independent express feelings perceptive helpful	guilt inadequacy vulnerability	allow mistakes take risks seeks approval
THE SCAPEGOAT	sullen defiant acting out chemical use blaming	hurt at not being heard loneliness	support of feelings acceptance challenge to be listened to confrontation

THE LOST CHILD	creative loners solitary withdrawn	loneliness rage encouragement	invitation consistency
THE MASCOT	hyperactive humor clumsy center of attention	fears not belonging fears breaking down needs information	physical touch taken seriously asked for input

The above chart gives a schematic view of the behaviors of the various survival roles of a family involved in alcohol addiction. Listed on the right are the needs for the specific people within the family system. The challenge for the family is to best use the continuum of care in order to re-receive the nurturance it needs. Also, because of the denial and the delusion that is an integral part of the illness, family members need outside help to determine and monitor their treatment plan.

The denial and the delusion of the alcoholic are almost proverbial. Stories abound of how difficult it was for someone to admit that they had a problem, that their life had become unmanageable. It is clear that the same degree of denial and delusion is present in the family members. The client is not just the one who has ingested the chemical who happens to have a family. The client is the chemically dependent family system. Families will get their needs met through counselors involving the family from Intervention preparation brought Recovery programs.

In other words, if the Chemically Dependent Person does not receive treatment, he will not likely recover. Without recovery, they will not change their abusive behaviors toward the family."

The Next Step

By now, you may have come to a decision you can live with, and are moving on mentally to plan your escape.

Once again, let's use the brainstorming form to list all of the parts of the problem: how can I safely leave my abuser? List all the aspects of the problem, and then group them together by area. Group-think solutions for each area, as before, then set out your plan in small doable steps.

22

Brainstorming Form – Leaving a battering Spouse

PROBLEMS:

SOLUTIONS:

Stepping Stones Flow Chart – Leaving a Battering Spouse

Beginning Now:

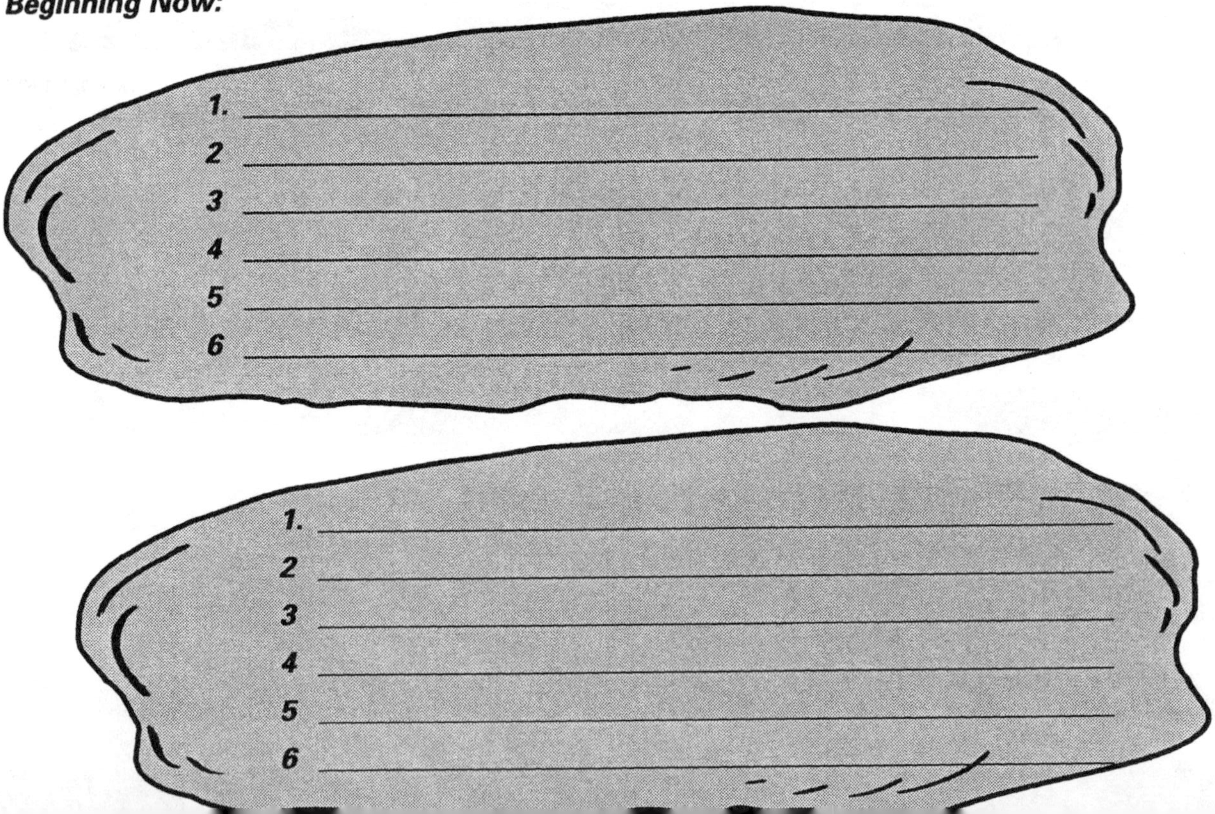

One Year Later!

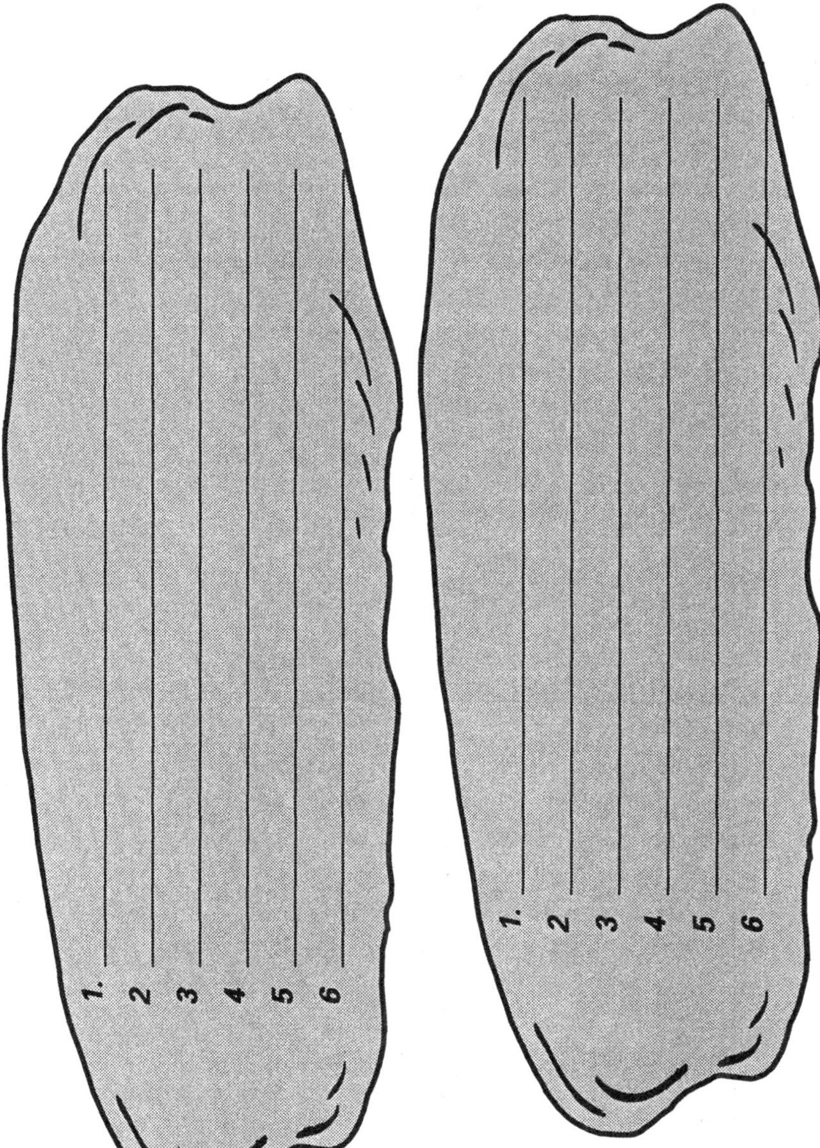

Documents You Will Need Before You Go

Gather the following documents and articles and put them together in a safe place where they won't be found. It will be easier to leave if you don't have to run out of the house with just the clothes on your back.

1. California Driver's License or Identification card and proof of legal status in the U.S.
2. Social Security cards for you and all children over three years old.
3. Current pictures of the entire family. (A picture of the batterer is useful for security reasons while at the shelter.)
4. Original birth certificates.
5. Proof of auto and health insurances.
6. Your children's immunization records (so they won't have to get the shots all over again at their new school.)
7. Credit cards, check book and last bank statement.
8. Money.
9. Extra clothing for you and the kids, especially shoes, which are in short supply at the shelters.
10. Kids school supplies, a few toys, and personal items.
11. Traveling alarm clock (to help you keep appointments for jobs and social services).
12. Your personal address book (do not leave this behind or he may harass your friends and family for your whereabouts).
13. A sewing kit for clothing repairs.
14. Prescription medicines for you and your kids.

Once you have a place available in a shelter, leave without announcing your intent. Don't threaten him with leaving or indicate your plans in any way, as this will alert him, making it impossible to make your escape.

And you are escaping from a prison of sorts. The batterer is a manipulative, power-starved person who needs to control others. If he will not let you go willingly, you must plan carefully and quietly. The basic idea boils down to: if you want to live; get ready; get set... and RUN. Get out of a bad relationship that will only become progressively worse over time.

Where To Go for Help

A brief resource guide for victims of domestic violence:

Alliance on Family Violence, Bakersfield	805-327-1091
Battered Women's Services, San Diego	619-234-3164
Desert Sanctuary, Barstow	619-256-3441
Domestic Violence Hotline	800-978-3600
Doves, Big Bear Lake	909-866-1546
East Los Angeles Shelter (24 hour Spanish)	213-268-7564
Every Woman's Shelter (24 hour Chinese, Japanese, Korean, Filipino and Vietnamese)	213-653-4042
Foothill Family Services	818-795-6907
Free Spirit Shelter, Los Angeles	213-937-1312
Haven Hills, San Fernando Valley	818-887-6589
Haven House, Pasadena	213-681-2626
Horizon House, Riverside	909-683-0829
House of Ruth, Pomona	909-988-5559
Human Options, South Laguna Beach	714-497-7017
Internal House, Seal Beach	310-594-4555
Jenesee Center, Los Angeles	213-731-6500
Los Angeles Battered Women's Hot line	310-392-8381
Option House, San Bernardino	909-381-3471
Phoenix House, Glendale	818-242-1106
Rainbow, San Pedro	310-547-9343
Santa Clarita Valley Battered Women's Assoc.	805-259-4357
1736 Family Crisis Center, Hermosa Beach	310-379-3620
Sojourn, Santa Monica	310-392-9896
So. Calif. Coalition for Battered Women (message)	213-655-6098
Su Casa, Lakewood (24 hour Spanish)	310-402-4888
Unity Home, Twenty-nine Palms	619-366-9663
Valley Oasis, Lancaster	805-945-6736
Wings, West Covina	818-966-0544
Woman Haven, El Centro	619-353-8530
Woman and Children's Crisis Shelter, Whittier	310-945-3937
Women's Transitional Living Center, Orange	714-992-1931
YWCA WINGS	818-967-0658
YWCA Womenshelter, Long Beach	310-437-4663

Chapter 6
Spousal Support Calculations

According to the *Divorce Handbook for California,* by Judge James W. Stewart, "the amount of spousal support is determined by the Family Code, which requires the judge to take certain factors into consideration." Some of the factors are:

1. the supporting party's ability to pay (is your spouse gainfully employed?)
2. the need to be supported in the style to which you have become accustomed (whether the amount will provide your previous standard of living)
3. the debts and assets of each person and the supported party's ability to be gainfully employed (do you earn the best income you possibly can?)

Another factor you should consider when asking for spousal support, is that it will be considered taxable income to you, so you must ask for enough money to compensate for the money the government will take out in taxes. Also, you cannot base the amount of your ex-spouse's income on the income of his new mate.

However, in a cruel twist of fate, the income of your new live-in lover can be taken into account in order to lower the payment you'll receive. (Suggestion: don't let a new man move in with you, at least not until your spousal support award is terminated.)

The length of the marriage usually determines the amount of time you're awarded spousal support. A long marriage is considered ten years or more, and is usually awarded more time and larger payments. (Suggestion: unless your spouse is abusive, you might opt for sticking it out the extra year in order to get a better settlement!)

Often, if you were a homemaker during the marriage, and can demonstrate the ability and motivation to go back to school, the judge may allow you extra time for your re-education before expecting you to go back to work.

Since the amount of your spousal support will depend on many factors, no real attempt has been made here to give you a certain dollar amount that you may expect. The truth of the matter is, you and your attorney, and your ex- spouse and his attorney can haggle over the amount all you want, but in the end, it is the judge who will decide. Since everyone has biases, you can either trust your future to luck and the decision of one judge, or you can ask for temporary support, while you prepare to do without your ex-husband's support payments.

Three Good Reasons Not to Depend On Spousal Support

1. If your ex quits his job or gets laid off, the payment can be reduced.
2. If the payment was based on a pre-1994 agreement, and included his new wife's income, the payment can be reduced.
3. If you decide to live with a new partner, his income can be taken into consideration in order to reduce your spousal support.

Think of your finances like a business. If you aren't making enough money, you can lower your expenses, raise your income or a combination of both. There is a very good reason that you should concentrate on increasing your income – ASAP!

A 1996 statute reads, "...the goal (of the State of California) is that the supported party shall be self-supporting within a reasonable period of time...which shall be considered one-half the length of the marriage." Therefore, it behooves you to upgrade your skills, degrees and experience in your chosen field, in order to make enough money to support yourself, rather than depending on spousal support.

Preparing To Get A Better/New Job

Here are some things that you can do to prepare yourself for a new job:

1. Update your resume. There are many books you can borrow from the library to help you set up your resume for a professional look. Try to type it on a computer, which can be rented in some copier shops and sometimes the local public library.
2. Start looking in the newspapers for the types of jobs you can apply for in the area you need to work in.
3. Increase or upgrade your job skills at a community college. Besides helping you update your skills, community college is one way to get inexpensive health care, access to a wonderful library system, discounts on movies and educational materials, psychological counseling and more.

4. Do an internship. This means offering to work for free for a short period of time. This will do a couple of things for you; basically it will get you in the door and let you know if you want to work in a certain industry.
5. To start out, get only one really killer outfit for interviews. Make it appropriate to the profession and you'll already look as though you belong there. Once I got a job as chiropractic assistant, because I wore a white coat to the interview. When the doctor walked into the waiting room, he assumed I already worked there!
6. Begin at a temporary job agency. For one thing, they test your skills and let you know what salary range you qualify for, and sometimes the agency may offer benefits. Many employers use temporary agencies to try out new employees before they decide to hire them full time. This allows *you* to check out the employer before you make a big move. You can learn what the employees and managers are really like, what kind of salaries are being paid to the permanent staff, and what kind of difficulties arise when working for the company.
7. Move on and don't look back. When you are finally ready to go onto your new job opportunity, don't worry about training your replacement. What I mean by this is, don't fall for one of the oldest traps women fall for which is: "The company will fall apart without you there", "No one else can be trusted," "No one else cares like you do," etc., etc. Some of the objections have a small basis in truth; however, it isn't healthy to believe that you are the only competent person in the world to do your job.

Chapter 7
Child Support Calculations

In *The Divorce Handbook* by Judge James W. Stewart, he describes his experience as a Santa Clara County judge. " I have presided over 24 financial disasters per week, or 1,250 per year. Although that is a small portion of the dissolution actions filed in Santa Clara County each year, they have a severe impact on those who have assets worth fighting over. Many of the 9500 filings result in either reconciliation or a settlement in which little is divided beyond some furniture and a couple of automobiles with scant value."

In other words, if you don't plan your divorce carefully, you may become impoverished. The basis for child support is determined by a mandatory statewide algebraic formula that is written into the California Family Code. It takes into consideration each parent's income and the time each spends with the children.

This information is then entered into the judge's computer program, and the computer provides a support figure for each child. Most people try to change the amount of the payment by fighting over the income information reported. Or, they disagree on the amount of time each parent really spends with each child.

Child support in California is now based solely on the parents' incomes; the courts do not consider a parent's expenses. The term "the feminization of poverty" began with child support and spousal support inequalities.

To change the amount of the payment a judge must find a "rebuttal factor", for example:

1. The custodial parent has the benefit of residing in the family residence that has a low mortgage payment compared with what a fair rent would be.
2. A parent's new mate has income that helps meet that parent's basic living expenses, thus making income available for the children.

New-Mate Income

The dispute over how much a parent is earning or should earn will continue to be the most volatile area in child support and spousal support issues. Each parent must bring income tax returns and recent, consecutive pay stubs to the hearing, to prove actual income.

Failing to Earn to Capacity is when one parent fails or refuses to earn to that parent's capacity and the other party seeks to prove that fact. For example, if your ex quits a high paying job to work at a lower income, you must be able to prove this in order to increase your payment.

Most of these issues must be discussed with your attorney; therefore it is your job to find a reliable, local attorney who is familiar with practices in the county, and the biases of individual judges in the county.

The issues of child care, health care, and private school expenses bear the potential to drastically increase the amount of child support a paying parent is required to pay to a custodial parent. Such sums are in addition to the basic child support set by schedule, and must be discussed prior to the award.

Chapter 8
Pet Custody Issues

This may seem ridiculous to some people, but most pet owners would agree that their pets are as dear to them as their own children. Many people consider them part of the family. So it may come as a shock to learn they are considered property by most states and are not "awarded" as in custody issues, but rather divided up with the pots and pans. The courts have long recognized and commented upon the tension between custody and property law when it comes to pets.

As cold as it may sound, you may need to prove ownership of your pet in order to keep it. For example, if you have receipts to show you paid for the pets from your own personal checking account, or receipts to show you took them to the veterinarian, training classes, etc., you can prove you are the primary owner of the pets. Some courts decide that possession of the family pet should be decided on a "best interest of the pet" foundation.

One of the first decisions considering the ownership of a dog was in 1944, regarding a Boston bull terrier that the husband had given an arbitrary value of $25.00. It seemed the husband was given the dog during the marriage as a gift from a veterinarian. The husband had then given the dog to the wife during the marriage, and she had been the primary caregiver.

This began an evolving body of law concerning "who gets Fluffy," which is based on who usually cares for a pet when making an ultimate division of marital property.

In a case in Texas (1981), the wife's evidence was that the dog was purchased with her separate funds, titled in her name, and remained in her possession up until the judgment of the court. In considering her case, the court was employing "a best interest of the pet" test. The court appointed the wife as the managing conservator of the parties' dog, then the court went on to state that dogs are property and must be treated as such. However, the court then concluded that the dog was the wife's property.

A court must first classify the pet as either marital property or separate property. The court may then consider whom could best care for the pet.

Consider a 1984 divorce case in Iowa, in which the husband gave the wife a dog for Christmas during the marriage. The Appellate court took issue with the characterization of the award of the dog as a custody matter. The court then classified the pet as marital property and issued award of the family dog to the husband, along with other items of personal property.

If the pet is owned before the marriage, the issue of equitable distribution of the pet (as in Bennett V. Bennett) is decided by the court in the favor of the husband, with visitation rights granted to the wife. This particular dog was the husband's premarital property, and thus the court disposed of the problem by finding that the dog was premaritally owned and therefore solely his property.

In Kansas (1997), the case of more than one pet, sharing of the pets was accomplished by awarding one pet to one party and another pet to the other party.

Once it is determined that the family pet is marital property, then the court may consider who could better care for the pet and who has the greater attachment to the pet. Your best bet in these cases is to collect up your receipts and figure out who owns the pet and who can best care for it. Whoever has primarily paid for the upkeep of the pet, taken it to the veterinarian, and spent the most time care-giving will most likely be named the owner.

Chapter 9
Planning Ahead to Make it Work

Being twice divorced myself; I know how hard it is to get to the point where you can emotionally handle the idea of getting divorced. But, in order to get a fair deal (an equitable settlement), you have to get to that point mentally. Whatever you have to do mentally and emotionally may take some time, so this is your assignment in the meantime:

Plan Ahead

1. You must be able to provide: receipts and credit card statements showing your purchases; cancelled checks for items you bought during the marriage; bank statements; CONTRACTUAL agreements you've signed; tax records (last 3 years); children's immunization/health records; your personal health records; birth certificates and marriage certificate. Keep all of these in a safe deposit box at the bank and you won't have to worry about having them lost or destroyed.
2. Think about where you will live. Will you stay in your current residence? If not, you will need to research your new neighborhood to find out if it is a safe area and near the schools you prefer/require for your children.

3. Will you need to change jobs? Update your resume and post it on the Internet, or contact a headhunter near you. Start checking out the classified ads, find out what the going wage is for your position.
4. Will you have a car or will you need to depend on public transportation? This will also affect where you can live. Some cities have reliable bus transportation, some do not.
5. Should you set up a separate credit card and checking account? Absolutely. If you do not have credit established in your name alone, it will be helpful to begin this process now.
6. Do you need to change your mailing address or get a Post Office box?
7. Get your budget under control! Lowering your expenses right away is easier and more realistic than increasing your income right away.
8. Get out of credit card debt.
9. Look at your lifestyle and consider eliminating luxury items in order to pay off larger debts like your house payments or credit card debt. Once these bills are paid, you'll have that extra chunk of money to save for the "inevitable emergency" or whatever else you may need.
10. Start building up your personal support network now. This is the time to join group activities, whether it's an exercise group, sports club, church group, volunteer organization, or a book club. Having fun and being active will keep you involved with people, and not always thinking about your own problems.
11. Have a plan. Start by brainstorming your problems, as described in *Chapter 1*, and come up with at least three solutions to each problem area. Then move on to the Stepping-Stones Form, which will help you plan things in smaller, do-able steps. Every three months, you can chart your progress, note your successes and re-strategize your shortcomings. We all encounter unforeseen obstacles, and it may take some time to knock them down, but you will.
12. Develop realistic expectations and goals for yourself and your children. Try to set goals you can achieve with the time and resources you have, so you can continue to experience success at solving problems, whether simple or complex.

A Last Thought

Because litigation is so expensive, it is better to settle your divorce out of court, if possible. This can be easier on your pocketbook than using the court system, because by the time all the experts have been paid, there is little left in your estate to fight over.

For this reason, I'm suggesting another route entirely. See if you can get an equitable resolution from your spouse, without attorneys. If not, you have to get whatever you can out of the marriage before it ends. This basically means paying off your car and credit card loans, so you can be free and clear, once you're divorced.

Brainstorming Form – My Obstacles to Leaving in One Year

PROBLEMS:

SOLUTIONS:

Stepping Stones Flow Chart – My Obstacles to Leaving in One Year –

Beginning Now:

1. ____________________
2 ____________________
3 ____________________
4 ____________________
5 ____________________
6 ____________________

1. ____________________
2 ____________________
3 ____________________
4 ____________________
5 ____________________
6 ____________________

One Year Later!

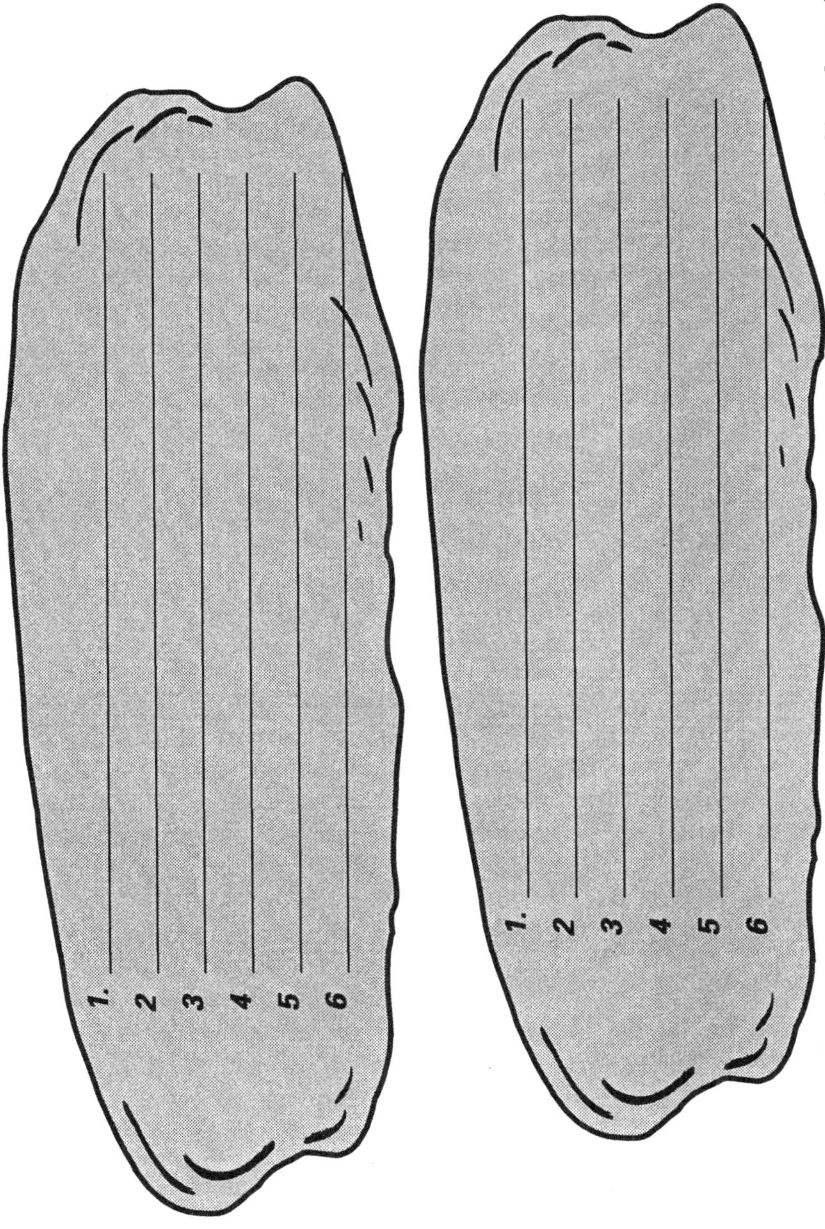

Chapter 10
After Limbo: Will You Go to Heaven or Hell?

Looking Forward to Your Future Relationship Without Dread

Understanding how hard it is to go through divorce, I wanted to end on a somewhat positive note. In my heart of hearts, when I was first married, I believed it was forever. I believed that marriage was the kind of thing you only do once. My parents never divorced.

When I found out my husband was cheating on me, I was devastated. Our sex life was great; we were active caring partners, yet he chose to go sleep with another woman. Why? What had I done wrong?

When I confronted him about the affair, he really didn't have any satisfactory answers.

"No, we weren't having marital, sexual, or emotional problems" and "no, he wasn't bored or unhappy with our sex together." He just had an itch he had to scratch, I guess. So, he agreed that he wouldn't sleep around again because it hurt my feelings and made me insanely angry. After the second and third time, I knew the guy was a philandering fool who would never change.

In my first divorce, I was young, without children and renting a house. We co-owned a car (which I gave him to facilitate his getting out of my life) and worked two separate jobs. We hadn't made any other major purchases except the car, so when I'd finally had enough, we packed our own personal belongings and went our separate ways. I must admit, this is the easiest type of divorce you can deal with, because:

1. We didn't own things we had to fight over.
2. We had no children.
3. He had hurt me so many times that I was over him emotionally by the time we parted.
4. We worked at separate places, so my income wasn't affected by the divorce.
5. I was healthy and able to work full time to support myself.

I went on my way, more angry than unhappy or lonely. I stayed single for a few years. I thought that just living alone for a while was enough to mend the harm done by the ex's cheating. Unfortunately, I instead wandered from man to man, until I found someone who would end up being worse for me than the first one. What followed was a short, bitter and physically violent 12 months I hope to never repeat in my life.

Without going into all the details here (See *Chapter 5*), I will say that the best advice from the counselors at the residential shelter for battered women was this: First fix the problem within yourself, then you will be the type of person to attract a healthier mate.

They suggest that a residential client wait one year after leaving the shelter before having an intimate relationship with someone. They also recommend that you continue with counseling for at least one year after leaving the shelter, in order to work out the inner issue that causes you to choose a partner who is harmful for you.

One piece of advice I'd like to add is, change your hunting patterns. In other words, if you usually meet men in nightclubs, try "fishing" at athletic or exercise clubs. If you've always done the chasing, wait until someone picks you. Breaking old patterns is an easy way to help you change your life.

This brings up one last observation that may help to change your perspective.

The Myth of The Perfect Mate

When you stop trying to be the perfect mate, and stop expecting someone else to be one, then you allow the possibilities for a real relationship to develop.

Stereotypes are double-edged swords, in that they hurt both the person who is trapped in an unwanted role, and the person who expects the stereotypical behavior. Some women have been raised to expect a man to come into their life and be the perfect romantic lover, gentle, compassionate and sensitive; a hardworking, physically strong, mentally sharp provider; a funny, kind friend; and a comfortable companion. This super person is also known as "The One." In other words, this poor individual is expected to be everything and its opposite for a woman.

These same unrealistic expectations are demanded of women who are expected to be sexual sirens in bed; patient, kind and loving as mothers; savvy, ambitious business people; and able to keep a perfectly spotless house!

In fact, it cripples our ability to identify a decent relationship when we're in one because it holds us to a level that no one person can attain for the other. It also causes us to chase after an impossible dream of a perfect romantic partner, ignoring the very real and solvable problems of most decent relationships. This expectation to fulfill our every need makes us unhappy with what we have, thinking only of what we lack in a relationship.

No one person can satisfy every need we have in our lives. We need a variety of relationships, from friends and family, to in-laws, acquaintances and business partners. Just as we wouldn't dream of limiting ourselves to one friend, we should not limit ourselves to one person for companionship. (This is not to say have more than one sexual companion, just other people you can share intimate thoughts with.)

If we could disarm this myth, and look to friends for companionship and discussions, as well as our mate, we would have fresh news and views to share instead of going over the same old ground. We should seek to expand our personal relationships to include more than one person to answer some of our emotional needs, instead of depending on one person for everything.

Happy at Last

While no story can have a completely "Pollyanna" ending, there is a happy ending to this story.

A man I met briefly before going into the residential battered women's shelter was asking my friend questions about me. He needed another roommate and asked her, "Does that cute, short girl with long brown hair, the one that you introduced me to a couple of months ago, need a place to stay?"

I did, and moved in as his roommate. Three months later we were on our way to becoming much more than just roommates. With five years to learn about each other's ways, we started trusting each other, and finally decided to tie the knot. Although some may say I'm foolhardy, as the old cliché reads: "Third time's a charm." And here we are, 17 years, 2 businesses, and several cats and dogs later, still together and still working at getting it right.

A good marriage takes a lot of work, but the benefits are clear. Take heart. You, too, can get through this and find the relationship that will work for you.

Glossary

Actuary	A statistician who computes insurance risks and premiums. (Source: *The American Heritage College Dictionary,* Third Edition 1997)
Assets	1. A useful or valuable quality, person or thing; an advantage or resource. 2. Assets, a. The entire property owned by a person, especially a bankrupt, that can be used to settle debts. (Source: *The American Heritage College Dictionary,* Third Edition 1997)
Brainstorm	1. A sudden clever plan or idea. To engage in or organize shared problem solving. (Source: *The American Heritage College Dictionary,* Third Edition 1997)
Budget	1. An itemized summary of expenditures for a given period along with proposals for financing them. 2. The total sum of money allocated for a particular purpose or period of time. (Source: *The American Heritage College Dictionary,* Third Edition 1997)
Cash Surrender Value of Life Insurance	The cash value of your life insurance policy, if you terminated your coverage.
Contractual	Of, relating to, or having the nature of a contract. (Source; *The American Heritage College Dictionary,* Third Edition 1997)

Deprogramming	Counteracting or trying to counteract the effect of an Indoctrination, esp. of a religion or cult. (Source: *The American Heritage College Dictionary,* Third Edition 1997)
Disposable Expenses	Things you buy that do not last more than one year, for example: clothes, food, magazine subscriptions, spa memberships, etc.
Dividends and Securities	Money earned from owning stocks and bonds.
Divest	1 (a) To deprive, as of rights or property; dispossess. (b) To be rid of, to sell or otherwise dispose of (a subsidiary company or investment). (Source: *The American Heritage College Dictionary,* Third Edition 1997)
Emotionally Independent	The aspect of our conscious that feels free from influence and the need for support from others to be whole.
Empower	To invest with power, especially legal power or official authority. (Source: *The American Heritage College Dictionary,* Third Edition 1997)
Enabler	To make activational, to operate, to supply with the means, knowledge, opportunity, to make able. (Source: *The American Heritage College Dictionary,* Third Edition 1997)
Equitable	Marked by or having equity, just and impartial. (Source: *The American Heritage College Dictionary,* Third Edition 1997)

Expenses	1 (a) Something spent to attain a goal or accomplish a purpose. (b) A loss for the sake of something gained; a sacrifice. 2. An expenditure of money; a cost. (Source: *The American Heritage College Dictionary,* Third Edition 1997)
Impoverished	1. Reduced to poverty; poverty-stricken. 2. Deprived of natural richness or strength. (Source: *The American Heritage College Dictionary,* Third Edition 1997)
Invested Expense	Things you buy that last more than one year, for example: a car, a home, computer equipment, an education.
Liability	1. Something for which one is liable; an obligation; a responsibility, or a debt. 2. Financial obligations. (Source: *The American Heritage College Dictionary,* Third Edition 1997)
Limbo	An intermediate place or state. (Source: *The American Heritage College Dictionary,* Third Edition 1997)
Mediator	One that mediates especially differences between disputes.(Source: *The American Heritage College Dictionary,* Third Edition 1997)
Proprietor	One who has legal title to something (an owner) of a business or any such establishment. (Source: *The American Heritage College Dictionary,* Third Edition 1997)
Quantify	To determine or express the quantity of. (Source: *The American Heritage College Dictionary,* Third Edition 1997)

Standard of living	Your standard of living is living in the style and comfort to which you are accustomed.
Subconscious	The part of the mind below conscious perception. (Source: *The American Heritage College Dictionary,* Third Edition 1997)

Diane Tegarden, a freelance writer living in Pasadena, is the owner/publisher of FireWalker Publications. She published her first work entitled "Getting OUT of Limbo–A Self-Help Divorce Book for Women," in April, 2004.

Tegarden has been a print journalist since 1992, covering a wide range of subjects including renewable energy, environmental concerns, holistic health, women's issues, and native spirituality.

Contact Diane Tegarden at:
www.firewalkerpublications.com

Other Books by Diane Tegarden

Light Through Shuttered Window
(Poetry)

Anti-Vigilante and The Rips in Time
(Science fiction)

Forthcoming:

Cami Chameleon, Sweet Hitchhiker

<u>Sources Cited</u>

Bepko, Claudia and Krestan, Jo Ann. *The Responsibility Trap.*

Haven House Training Manual. California. 1985.

Nicarthy, Jenny. *Getting Free.*

Stewart, James W. Divorce *Handbook for California,* Fourth Edition.

California. Impact Publishers, Inc. 1999.

Wegscheider, Sharon. *From the Family Trap to Family Freedom.*

Alcoholism.

Background Reference:

Chatzky, Jean Sherman. "Money Smart, A dollar here a dollar there." *USA Weekend.* May 17-19, 2002.

"How to Pay Less for Almost Everything." *Reader's Digest,* June 2002, p71-79.

"Marriage Enrichment Groups", http://mentalhelp.net/psyhelp/chap10/chap10n.htm. 06/14/02

"Property and Debt Division", http://www.nolo.com/lawcenter/ency/article.cfm/.../. 08/09/02

CPSIA information can be obtained
at www.ICGtesting.com
Printed in the USA
BVHW031353190220
572802BV00001B/105

9 780974 536934